JOEL CHANDLER HARRIS—FOLKLORIST

JOEL CHANDLER HARRIS
—FOLKLORIST

by

STELLA BREWER BROOKES

THE UNIVERSITY OF GEORGIA PRESS
ATHENS

PRINTED IN THE UNITED STATES OF AMERICA

To the Memory

of

E. Luther Brookes

PREFACE

"Cum down ter dat, . . . an' dey ain't nuffin' dat aint cu'us."

—Uncle Remus: His Songs and His Sayings

It does seem specially curious that of all the articles written about Harris, strangely enough there is left untouched an analysis of the folklore in his Uncle Remus books. The purpose of the present volume is to supply this lack.

As the subject has shaped itself, it has seemed convenient to arrange it in two parts. Although Harris's intellectual world was a small one, his literary box of make-up limited and his properties few, it seemed advisable to give the background—environmental and literary—to which the writing and publication of the Uncle Remus books are ascribable. Part I, then, deals with material assembled concerning the influences which were most potent in his early years prior to the publication of the first Uncle Remus book in 1880.

Part II may claim to be an innovation. Here an analysis is given of the folklore in the ten volumes. The classifications embodied in the present study are my own, based upon a detailed examination of the productions. The chief task here was to study the material carefully arranged under the captions of Trickster Tales, Myths, Supernatural Tales, Proverbs, Dialect, and Songs.

ACKNOWLEDGMENTS

In preparing this manuscript I have necessarily had to seek the advice and help of others. It is a genuine pleasure to acknowledge here the guidance and scholarly assistance of Dr. Harold Thompson, Cornell University, Ex-President of the American Folklore Society, under whose direction this volume was prepared and to whom any acknowledgment is inadequate as compared to the valuable aid given. For analytical reading of the manuscript, I am indebted to Professor M. H. Abrams of Cornell University and Professor Walter Mackellar of New York University. Further help, graciously and efficiently accorded, was secured from Mrs. Julia Collier Harris, daughter-in-law of Joel Chandler Harris, who read the manuscript meticulously, gave permission to draw freely from her books (debts specifically itemized elsewhere), and aided and encouraged me in many other valuable ways. Thanks are also due Mr. Julian La Rose Harris, eldest son of Joel Chandler Harris, who read the material critically and was exceedingly helpful in certain matters pertaining to information which he had firsthand from his father. Dr. Thomas H. English, Curator of the Harris Collection at Emory University, called attention to important omissions from the original manuscript and courteously co-operated in the use of all available material on Harris. To my brother, J. Mason Brewer, who first stimulated my interest in folklore, may be credited the enthusiasm for undertaking this research. Finally, I am indebted in the preparation of the manuscript for aid of a technical nature which went far beyond that in interest, intelligence, and accuracy, to Mrs. Ruby Arnold, Miss Sara Perry, Mrs. Ruth Perry Scott, and Miss Wilhelmina Gilbert.

TABLE OF CONTENTS

INTRODUCTION

Certainly no American needs to be introduced to the beloved Georgian, Joel Chandler Harris. There is no doubt that the Uncle Remus stories head the list of our country's folktales, and there should be no doubt that their author must be included in the roster of the dozen American writers who have contributed most to the world's literature. Even Georgia, which has been accustomed to literary honors from the time of Longstreet through the days of Lanier and down to the present pupil age, must take a special pride in Mr. Harris.

After his lamented death it was obvious that at least two books about him must be written, but until the completion of the present volume only one has appeared. The first need, a sympathetic biography by one who knew him well personally, was superbly met in 1918 by *The Life and Letters of Joel Chandler Harris*, composed by the author's gifted daughter-in-law, Mrs. Julia Collier Harris. The second volume desired was an account of Harris the folklorist. It might have been a scientific study of the parallels between the Uncle Remus tales and folktales found in Africa, but the two or three scholars properly equipped to discuss African lore were otherwise engaged. Fortunately a book of much wider appeal, not to the scientist but to all lovers of Uncle Remus, has appropriately been completed by an Atlantan. It is exactly what was needed most: an account of the author's own idea of folklore and an analysis of his tales, proverbs, and songs by types.

Mrs. Stella Brewer Brookes is a graduate of Wiley College, a Master of Arts of the University of Michigan, and a Doctor of Philosophy of Cornell University where I had the pleasure of directing her studies. She is the sister of another well-known folklorist, Professor J. Mason Brewer.

In 1924 she became a resident of Atlanta and Chairman of the Department of English at Clark College. Her grace of manner, her fine literary taste, and her charming sense of humor are quite as important for her task as the scholarship which is never intrusive but always present.

It seems symbolic and gratifying that this tribute to Mr. Harris represents the cordial co-operation of his family, the generously granted aid of the Harris Collection at Emory University, the admirable presswork of the University of Georgia and the informed zeal of a Southern scholar. All these advantages which Mrs. Brookes has enjoyed remind me of a story which Mrs. Joel Chandler Harris—née Esther La Rose of Lansingburg near Albany, New York—told to my little son years ago. He had just declared, in the words of Uncle Remus, "I bleedz to do that." With her gentle smile Mrs. Harris said: "Arthur, once somebody scolded Mr. Harris for making Brer Rabbit climb a tree. 'Well,' said my husband, 'you see the houn' dogs were after Brer Rabbit, and he was just bleedz to climb that tree.' " Obviously Mrs. Brookes was bleedz to write this book, a tribute to a great and good man from one who represents the people whom he loved.

Harold W. Thompson
Ex-President, The American Folklore Society.

Cornell University.

Key to Abbreviations

Brer Rabbit:	Joel Chandler Harris, *Uncle Remus and Brer Rabbit.*
Daddy Jake:	Joel Chandler Harris, *Daddy Jake, the Runaway and Short Stories Told After Dark.* (1896 edition).
Editor and Essayist:	Julia Collier Harris, *Joel Chandler Harris, Editor and Essayist.*
Friends:	Joel Chandler Harris, *Uncle Remus and His Friends.*
Life and Letters:	Julia Collier Harris, *Joel Chandler Harris, Editor and Essayist.*
Little Boy:	Joel Chandler Harris, *Uncle Remus and the Little Boy.*
Nights:	Joel Chandler Harris, *Nights with Uncle Remus.*
Returns:	Joel Chandler Harris, *Uncle Remus Returns.*
Seven Tales:	Joel Chandler Harris, *Seven Tales of Uncle Remus.*
S. *and* S.:	Joel Chandler Harris, *Uncle Remus: His Songs and His Sayings.* (1880 edition)
Tar-Baby:	Joel Chandler Harris, *The Tar-Baby and Other Rhymes.*
Told By:	Joel Chandler Harris, *Told By Uncle Remus.*

"Dat's a tale, honey, an' tellin' tales is playin'."

—*Uncle Remus and His Friends.*

"It's mighty funny 'bout tales . . . . Tell um ez you may an' whence you may, some'll say tain't no tale, an' den ag'in some'll say dat it's a fine tale. Dey ain't no tellin'. Dat de reason I don't like ter tell no tale ter grown folks, speshually ef dey er white folks. Dey'll take it an' put it by de side er some yuther tale what dey got in der min' an' dey'll take on dat slonchidickler grin what allers say, "Go way, man! You dunner what a tale is!" An' I don't—I'll say dat much fer ter keep some un else fum sayin 'it."

—*Told by Uncle Remus.*

I

THE WRITING AND PUBLICATION OF THE UNCLE REMUS STORIES

I

ENVIRONMENTAL AND LITERARY INFLUENCES

AMONG THE IMMORTAL "REAL FOLKS" OF LITERATURE Uncle Remus's place is secure; in the ancient order of story-tellers his fame is international. This figure which Joel Chandler Harris added to the gallery of literary portraits is as much a part of world literature as Rip Van Winkle or the inimitable Micawber.

Some men's writings are the greatest part of them, and posterity studies their lives through a spirit of curiosity excited by their works. In a sense this is true of Harris, but in a larger sense one studies his life to find those forces, environmental and literary, which motivated his productions. Seldom in literary history has there been so unconscious a lapsing into literary expression; seldom has there been an author so amazed at sudden fame. Critics have justly acclaimed him the greatest interpreter of the Negro in the period which Uncle Remus has so aptly described as " . . . befo' de war, endurin' er de war, en atterwads." Yet this unexcelled portrayer of the Negro, this matchless writer of the difficult art of the spoken word, had very few advantages of education.

What Harris did have was an impulse to write—strong, fresh, and inevitable. When the opportunity came he seemed peculiarly fitted by temperament and environment to delight the world with some old stories of potent charm. He had no vaulting ambition to satisfy; he never consciously strove for success. He had some familiar stories to tell which he had listened to in the cabins of the Negroes—stories which many knew but few had the art to re-tell skillfully—and he told them as simply and naturally as if he were talking. He told them because he enjoyed telling them. Seldom in the history of mankind have so many had so much pleasure from one man's enjoyment. His mission was to make people happy. He expresses his delight at having added something to the world's store of happiness in the dedication of the Frost edition of the Remus Stories:

> I seem to see before me the smiling faces of thousands of children—some young and fresh, and some wearing the friendly marks of age, but all children at heart—and not an unfriendly face among them . . . and while I am trying hard to speak the right word, I seem to hear a voice lifted above the rest, saying: "You have made some of us happy." And so I feel my heart fluttering and my lips trembling, and I have to bow silently and turn away, and hurry back into the obscurity that fits me best.[1]

No attempt will be made to give details of his life. Characteristic incidents will be stated which furnished the background and made up the wealth of material which later found expression in his folklore. Any student of Harris is under a heavy debt to his daughter-in-law, Julia Collier Harris, for complete biographical information.[2] Other members of the Harris family have furnished significant facts,[3] and columnists and historians have supplied material that is helpful.

The materials for his folklore were chiefly ascribable to the environment which surrounded him. He was born in the small village of Eatonton, Putnam County, Georgia. His mother was poor, and had been deserted by his father, but did her utmost to rear the boy as well as circumstances afforded. Harris was a small, wiry, red-headed, freckled-faced lad, with a tendency to stutter. Though shy and reticent among those whom he did not know, he was a fun-loving, joke-playing fellow among his associates. He attended the day school at Eatonton until he was twelve years old; then the incident occurred that gave him the opportunity which proved so important to him in later years, his employment by Mr. Turner of the "Turnwold Plantation." However, he never forgot the kindness of the people among whom he spent his earliest days. He wrote:

> It was a great blessing for a young fellow in the clutches of poverty to be raised up among such people as those who lived in Eatonton when I was a boy. . . . I have not the slightest difficulty in the world in referring all that I have done or hope to do to the kindly interest which the people of Eatonton took in my welfare when I was too young to know anything of the difficulties of life or the troubles that inhabit the world by right of discovery and possession. But Eatonton was not a newspaper office, and I had to leave there in order to stick my head in an ink fountain. There came a time when I had to be up and doing, as the poet says, and it so happened that I was in the post office at Eatonton reading the Milledgeville papers when the first number of the "Countryman" was deposited on the counter where all the newspapers were kept. I read it through, and came upon an advertisement which announced that the editor wanted a boy to learn the printer's trade. This was my opportunity, and I seized it with both hands. I wrote to the editor, whom I knew well, and the next time he came to town he sought me out, asked if I had written the letter with my own hand, and in three words the bargain was concluded.[4]

Thus, Harris left Eatonton and set forth on what turned out to be the most important journey of his life.

He accompanied Mr. Turner to his plantation, "Turnwold," which was also in Putnam County. It was a large and beautiful estate flanked by forests of great value. The immense wildwood that environed the plantation, as well as Mr. Turner's library and the printing office of *The Countryman,* became the school for the impressionable young man.

When Harris was employed on *The Atlanta Constitution,* years after he had left "Turnwold," he wrote:

> In the history of American journalism, as strange as the statement may seem, there has been but one country newspaper. . . . It was published in the state of Georgia, county of Putnam, nine miles from any post office or town and its success was wholly dependent upon the individuality of its editor. It originated in the desire on the part of the Southern gentleman of ample means and large culture to address the people on matters of large concern. The name of this unique little publication was *The Countryman,* and it was published upon the plantation of Mr. J. A. Turner, nine miles from Eatonton. In the prospectus printed in the first number which was issued in the Spring of 1862, it was announced that *The Countryman* would be modelled after Addison's little paper, "The Spectator", and Goldsmith's little paper, *The Bee,* and for a while the promise of the prospectus was fulfilled. But *The Countryman* gradually grew even beyond the anticipation of its editor. It became immensely popular, was enlarged, and, suiting himself to the demands of a larger and less cultivated audience, the style of the editor became less intensely literary, until finally he came to write almost entirely in what Mr. James R. Randall, the poet, who is quite a dandy among *litterateurs,* called "the choice of Georgia dialect." [5]

He describes the office of the newspaper as being very small and the hand-press as old and worn, but he quickly mastered the boxes of the printer's cases and became of valuable assistance to Mr. Snelson—foreman, operator, and pressman. Though he was tremendously interested in the work on the newspaper, fortunately it did not require all of his time. It was generally completed in the mornings, and the evenings he spent either reading in Mr.

Turner's library or visiting the Negroes in company with the Turner children.

The strongest traits of Harris are sympathy and humor. His characters are great because of the lifelike guise in which they are presented. It was during the four years on the "Turnwold Plantation" that the impressions were made which were later released in his stories. He was vigilant of the life about him. He had the gift of appreciating the deep emotional side of the people, and he learned at first hand the habits of the animal creatures whom he later vested with such personal traits. From the window of the printing shop he watched the blue jays build their nests, and frequently the gray fox came near his window. Near the printing press a partridge and her mate built their nest. In the afternoons and evenings he liked to hunt rabbits and possums, and nothing thrilled him more than rounding up the harriers for a fox-hunt or in pursuit of "old zip coon."

In *On the Plantation,* Harris presents vivid memories of the years spent at "Turnwold." Not only does he tell of evenings spent around the fireside, but he relates other events—adventurous, jolly, pathetic. From these contacts he learned the lesson of good will, and there was opened to him the heart of the Negro which he read studiously. Outstanding among these incidents was his meeting with Mink, the Negro slave who because of ill treatment had run away and was forced to steal to satisfy his hunger. A few excerpts from that first meeting will be given to show something of Harris's sympathetic sensitiveness.

"Run, John," exclaimed Mrs. Snelson; "I just know somebody is stealing my dominicker hen and her chickens. Run!"

"Let the lad go," said Mr. Snelson, amiably. "He's young and nimble, and whoever's there he'll catch 'em."

[Joe reached the hen-house and in groping his way around laid his hand on somebody.]

"Who are you?" he asked . . . .

"Is dis de little marster what come fum town ter work in de paper office?"

"Yes; who are you, and what are you doing here?"

"I'm name Mink, suh, an' I b'longs to Marse Tom Gaither. I bin run'd away an' I got dat hongry dat it look like I bleedz ter ketch me a chicken. I bin mighty nigh famished, suh. I wish you'd please, suh, excusen me dis time."

"Why didn't you break and run when you heard me coming?" asked Joe, who was disposed to take a practical view of the matter.

"You wuz dat light-footed, suh, dat I ain't hear you, an' sides dat, I got my han' kotch in dish yer crack, an' you wuz right on top er me 'fo' I kin work it out."

"Well, get your hand out and stay here till I come back, and I'll fetch you something to eat . . . ."

[Harris then went to the house and said to Mr. Snelson:]

"It's all right, sir," . . . "None of the chickens are gone."

"A great deal of fuss and no feathers," said Mr. Snelson. "I doubt but it was a mink."

"Yes," said Joe laughing. "It must have been a Mink, and I'm going to set a bait for him."

Joe got three biscuits and a pone of cornbread and carried them to Mink . . . .

"God bless you little marster!" cried Mink.[6]

In many ways the Negroes played an important role in Harris's life. From the time that he had manifested this kindness toward Mink, he observed that all the Negroes who were Mink's friends were especially considerate of him—willing to do many favors for him. The secret of it was explained by Harbert, the "man-of-all-work" around the "big house".

"Marse Joe," said Harbert one day, "I wuz gwine 'long de road de udder night an' I met a great big nigger man. Dish yer nigger man took an' stop me, he did, an' he 'low, 'dey's a little white boy on yo' place which I want you fer ter keep yo' two eyes on 'im, an' when he say come, you come, 'an when he say go, you go.' I 'low, 'Hey, big nigger man! what de matter?' an' he 'spon' back, 'I done tole you, an' I ain't gwine tell you no mo'.' So dar you got it, . . . an' dat de way it stan's."[7]

So it was that these humble people smoothed many a rough place for Harris and showered upon him many courtesies. Shy among many other people, he seemed to feel free and happy when associating with them. He came to know them intimately, and during these days he unconsciously absorbed their fables and their ballads; he listened intently to the soft elisions of their dialect, the picturesque imagery of their speech, the undertones and overtones of their mellifluous voices; and, as a result of this close observation, to him will always belong the honor of presenting to the public the most accurate record of the dialect of that transient era.

Harris also heard stories of "patter-rollers", of deserters, and of runaways. Another meeting with Mink probably furnishes some insight into his early impressions of stories and the art of telling them. One day when he had been hunting rabbits, he wandered until night and was lost in the woods. He sought shelter in an old cabin. Later, two other people entered the cabin and thinking it unoccupied began talking. Among the things of which one of them talked was the kindness of the little white boy who worked on the paper. Harris recognized one of the voices as that of Mink. He decided to have some fun; so in a voice that sounded as if it were a voice from the grave, he said: "I want Mink; I want Mink." He had heard through the conversation that the name of the other character was Injun Bill, so he repeated his weird cry, "I want Injun Bill." The two men became so alarmed that they fell upon each other. Harris laughed aloud and revealed himself. During the time they were conversing, two other persons, deserters from the army, came in the cabin seeking shelter. To pass the time away the members of the group told stories. Mink told the story of "Ole Mammy Sheep." The most interesting stories were related by Injun Bill. Mink had no admiration for the rabbit of the Indian; in Injun Bill's story, "Brer Rabbit and the Overcoat," the rabbit could not fool the other animals and make them think he was a beaver although he had on a beaver's coat. The animals discovered his disguise and punished him by splitting his upper lip with a sharp flint rock. At the conclusion of the story Mink said:

> "Shoo! Dat Injun rabbit. Nigger rabbit would 'a' fooled dem creeturs right straight along, an' he wouldn't 'a' bin cotch nudder."[8]

The materials and backgrounds for Harris's folklore came, as we have seen, from the plantation and its environs. Let us turn now to the literary interests and motivations. As a boy he was fascinated by one book which made an indelible impression upon him. In a literary biography, "An Accidental Author," which he wrote for *Lippincott's Magazine*, he says:

> My desire to write—to give expression to my thoughts—grew out of hearing my mother read *The Vicar of Wakefield*. I was too young to appreciate the story, but there was something in the humor of that remarkable little book that struck my fancy, and I straightway fell to composing little tales, in which the principal character—whether hero or heroine—silenced the other characters by crying, *Fudge!* at every possible opportunity. None of these little tales have been preserved, but I am convinced that since their keynote was *Fudge!* they must have been very close to human nature.[9]

He reaffirmed his interest in this same book in a letter to William Baskervill, dated April 15, 1895, in which he said:

> The first book that attracted my attention, and the one that held it longest, was and is *The Vicar of Wakefield*. The only way to describe my experience with that book is to acknowledge that I am a crank. It touches me more deeply—it gives me the "all-overs" more severely—than all others. Its simplicity, its air of extreme wonderment—have touched and continue to touch me deeply. Apart from this all good books have interested me.[10]

Perhaps in addition to the appeal of the humor to which

Harris has referred, there was also the deep human sympathy of the book which found a response in one of such generous sympathy and understanding.

Harris had early shown a desire and inclination to write. It was that impulse which led him to leave Eatonton and take up residence at "Turnwold". It was during his experiences there that he began scribbling and the primal impulse to see some of his expressions in print seized him. He gives an account of his management of these early newspaper brevities:

While setting type for *The Countryman,* I contributed surreptitiously to the columns of that paper, setting my articles from the 'case' instead of committing them to paper, and thus leaving no evidence of authorship. I supposed that this was a huge joke; but, as Mr. Turner read the proof of every line that went into his paper, it is probable that he understood the situation and abetted it.[11]

Later he became more courageous and submitted some of his work to Mr. Turner. The editor scrutinized it frankly and criticized it severely. However, he believed him to have talent and was convinced of the young man's unusual interest in writing. Thus, he became Harris's literary adviser. Julia Harris prints a note which was found in an old scrapbook:

For the first time since you sent in this article, I have found time to examine it, and though it has merit, I regret that I have to reject it, because it is not up to the standard of the "Countryman". In the first place, you have made a bad selection in the article you have chosen for a subject. That article is contemptible and beneath criticism. It borders on idiocy. Captain Flash did his paper injustice in publishing it. In the next place, there is want of unity and condensation in your article. It is headed, "Irishmen—Tom Moore," and then goes off on a great variety of subjects, and is too diffuse on everything it touches.

In writing hereafter,

1st, select a good—a worthy subject.

2nd, stick to that subject.

3rd, say what you have to say in as few words as possible. Study the "nervous condensation" which you so much admire in Captain Flash. All this is for your good.

J. A. Turner

Aug. 21st, 1864.[12]

Mr. Turner was one of the first journalists to recognize the important use to which the Negro could be put in American literature. In *The Countryman*, December 22, 1862, he wrote:

I do emphatically wish us to have a Southern literature. And prominent in our books I wish the negro placed. The literature of any country should be a true reflex in letters of the manners, customs, institutions and local scenery of that country . . . . Let us write about things at home and round them.[13]

In 1879 an article written by Harris for *The Atlanta Constitution* seemed to reiterate what his benefactor had earlier written:

The very spice and essence of all literature, the very marrow and essence of all literary art is its localism. No literary artist can lack for materials in this section. They are all here around him, untouched, undeveloped, undisturbed, unique and original, as new as the world, as old as life, as fair as flowers, as beautiful as the dreams of genius. But they must be mined; they must be run through the stamp mill. Where is the magician who will catch them and store them up? . . . We have no Southern literature worthy of the name, because an attempt has been made to give to it the peculiarities of sectionalism rather than to impart to it the flavor of localism.[14]

Throughout Harris's writings are innumerable proverbs, proverbial expressions, philosophical and witty sayings. There is a possibility that he was first inspired by this type of literature from inclusions in *The Countryman* of excerpts from Percy's *Anecdotes* and Rochefoucauld's *Maxims*. Harris mentions these productions in a comment on the contents of the paper:

Another feature of the "Countryman" was the fact that there

was never any lack of copy for the foreman and the apprentice to set. Instead of clipping from his exchanges the editor sent to the office three books from which extracts could be selected. These books were *Lacon,* Percy's *Anecdotes,* and Rochefoucauld's *Maxims.*[15]

As has been said, Harris's own command of a clear, pure English and his conviction that a writer must look to life around him for materials, he owed largely to Turner; but examples of the actual use of local material came through another channel. It was Irwin Russell who asked, "Is there not poetry in the character of the negro?" and who demonstrated the rich source for Southern writers. His influence on Harris cannot be passed over lightly, for it was he who first faithfully and skillfully presented the Negro in literary portraiture. Harris acknowledges Russell's priority in this field in the Introduction which he wrote to a volume of Russell's poems, published in 1888:

> Irwin Russell was among the first—if not the very first—of Southern writers to appreciate the literary possibilities of negro character, and of the unique relations existing between the two races before the war, and was among the first to develop them. The opinion of an uncritical mind ought not to go for much, but it seems to me that some of Irwin Russell's negro-character studies rise to the level of what, in a large way, we term literature. His negro operetta, "Christmas-Night in the Quarters," is inimitable. It combines the features of a character study with a series of bold and striking plantation pictures that have never been surpassed. In this remarkable group,—if I may so term it,—the old life before the war is reproduced with a fidelity that is marvelous.
>
> But the most wonderful thing about the dialect poetry of Irwin Russell is his accurate conception of the negro character. The dialect is not always the best,—it is often carelessly written,—but the negro is there, the old-fashioned, unadulterated negro, who is still dear to the Southern heart. There is no straining after effect—indeed, the poems produce their result by indirection; but I do not know where could be found to-day a happier or a more perfect representation of negro character.[16]

To Russell then goes the distinction of being the leading pioneer in the field, not merely because he first caught the general attention of the reading public by his Negro dialect poems published in the eighteen-seventies, but because he stimulated others to work in this new, fertile field of literary material. Indeed he laid bare the field in which Harris discovered inestimable treasures. So *The Vicar of Wakefield, The Countryman,* J. A. Turner, and Irwin Russell constitute significant formative influences in the budding career of Harris.

The aforementioned influences presumably might have led indirectly to the writing of the Uncle Remus Series of stories, but Harris himself tells us the direct influence in an article which he contributed to an "Experience Meeting" of writers in *Lippincott's Magazine.* Under the title of "An Accidental Author," this is what he wrote in part:

> *The Countryman* was published on a plantation, and it was on this and neighboring plantations that I became familiar with the curious myths and animal stories that form the basis of the volumes accredited to Uncle Remus. I absorbed the stories, songs, and myths that I had heard, but had no idea of their literary value until, sometime in the seventies, *Lippincott's Magazine* printed an article on the subject of negro folklore, containing rough outlines of some of the stories. This article gave me my cue, and the legends told by Uncle Remus are the result . . . .
>
> This was the accidental beginning of a career that has been accidental throughout. It was an accident that I went to *The Countryman,* an accident that I wrote "Uncle Remus", and an accident that the stories put forth under that name struck the popular fancy.[17]

The article by William Owens to which Harris refers appeared in December, 1877, under title of "Folk-lore of Southern Negroes."[18] Harris wrote an editorial in *The Atlanta Constitution* about this issue of *Lippincott's Magazine* of December, 1877; what he said with reference to the Owens article is well worth noting:

. . . Wm. Owens contributes an article on "Folk-lore of the Southern Negroes" which is remarkable for what it omits rather than for what it contains. The author is even at a loss to account for the prefix, "Buh"—as he puts it—which the negroes give to the animals who figure in their stories, as "Buh Rabbit", "Buh Wolf" etc. We judge from the tone of Mr. Owens' article that he is familiar only with the lore of the nondescript beings who live on the coast, otherwise he would have no difficulty in determining the derivation of the word "buh". The real Southern negro pronounces the word as though it were written "brer" and he confines its use to the animals themselves—for instance: "Den bimeby, Mr. Fox, he see Mr. Rabbit comin' 'long, an' he say, 'howdy Brer Rabbit—how you gittin' 'long dese days?' " It is unquestionably a contraction of the word, "brother". But enough of this . . . .[19]

"Enough of this," Harris said in the editorial, but it seems as if this were just the beginning of his ventures in folklore. The article set in motion a train of thought that brought back graphically moments and experiences of his youth. It opened his eyes to the value of those early contacts. Owens, instead of inspiring by way of example, whetted by way of omission. To Harris, Owens's portrayal seemed feeble, inaccurate, lifeless. In his own mind there began to take shape the tales as they were actually told, the dialect as it was actually spoken.

From this point dates his literary awakening. It was later that a kind Fate brought the folklore from his mental store-house to the printed page. To summarize—the picturesque panorama of the plantation furnished Harris with his materials; the instruction of Mr. Turner stimulated his ambition and developed his talent for writing; Goldsmith's sympathetic portrayal of human nature heightened his interest in people; Irwin Russell demonstrated the possibility of character delineation through the medium of dialect; William Owens awakened and aroused him to the literary value of folk-tales.

The environment and journalistic tradition of Harris

reinforced his natural gift for humor. Indeed, it is frequently as a humorist rather than as a folklorist that Harris is studied; certainly, one of the most delightful features of the Uncle Remus stories is their humor.

Possibly few American humorists have been funny in appearance, but Harris was. Julia Harris tells of the impression which he made when first introduced to his companions of the Savannah *Morning News*. The first night that the editor brought him into the composing room the men thought him "the greenest, gawkiest-looking specimen of humanity" that they had ever seen. They wanted to know, "What was the critter Colonel Estill had found? Was it human or what?" When informed that he was the new paragrapher, the query came, "How did the Colonel catch him—in a fish-trap or a net?" Small of stature, red-haired, freckled-faced, with an impediment in his speech, Harris was made the object of many jokes. However, he was a jokester himself, so he took them rather good-naturedly. His friends used colorful adjectives to describe him. "Pink-Top", "Red-Top", "Our friend of the ensanguined fore-top", "Molasses-haired Humorist", "Vermilion-Pate", "Naughty Boy of the Savannah *Morning News*", were some of the nicknames bestowed upon him. His paragraphs, copied all over the State, were reproduced under such titles as: "Harrisgraphs", "Red-Top Flashes", "Harris-Sparks", "Hot Shots from Red-Hair-Is".[20]

Colleagues sometimes protested against the frequent references to Harris's red hair. One wrote, "Whenever our friend Harris makes a hit at any of the State papers, the editor of the worsted journal invariably falls back on that old, stale, weather-beaten and worn out repartee, 'red head'. J. C. has one consolation—if his hair *is* red, it is a durned sight *more than* their articles are."[21] Another wrote, "Why is the red-headed department of the

'News' like the tail of a dog? Because that's where the wag is."[22]

Despite the jokes, Harris's talent was readily recognized and many tributes were paid him during the time of his employment on the Savannah *Morning News*. One or two will serve to illustrate the esteem in which he was held. The editor of one Georgia paper wrote:

> What shall we say of the bright, sparkling, vivacious, inimitable Harris? There is no failing in his spirit of wit and humor, playful raillery and pungent sarcasm. As a terse and an incisive paragraphist, he is unequalled in the South. One wonders at times that his fund of quips and odd fancies does not occasionally become exhausted, but the flow continues from day to day without sign of dimunition or loss of volume; J. C. Harris is a genius of rare and versatile abilities.[23]

Another said of him:

> Harris is the wit of the press. There is nothing waspish or malicous in the little bon-mots he showers upon the heads of his contemporaries, day after day. They are pure, chaste, and sparkling, with scarcely more of harm in them but much more of brilliancy, than the shining drops of a June day rain. When he gets his hump up, however, and wants to help the "Colonel" drive an issue home, he puts an edge to his paragraphs and they whistle through the air with the emphasis of a November sleet storm.[24]

Harris was a creature of paradoxes like many other geniuses. He was morbidly sensitive, incurably modest and shy, and refused to make public appearances or read publicly any of the stories which he had written—he did not read the stories even to his own children. Yet among friends and colleagues in informal conversation, he was the jolliest of the group. Sometimes the jokes he would tell were so droll and true to nature that his audience and himself would be convulsed. His sense of humor was always creeping out, frequently at unexpected times and places. There was the time when he left Savannah on account of the fever raging there, came to Atlanta, and registered at Kimball House: "J. C. Harris. one wife, two bow-legged children and a bilious nurse." He was the source of so much fun during his stay at the Kimball House that the proprietor made no charges, saying that he thought it was he who was indebted to Harris. There was the time at the Florida House in Savannah when Harris urged a friend to play a prank on one of their fellow boarders. The person was a very serious and sober man, but one night when he was returning to the house, Harris said to his friend, "Let's have some fun." They caught the gentleman by each arm and proceeded to assist him to the house and up the stairs, waking all the boarders with their exclamations of solicitude for the apparently drunken man. The man protested in vain. There were the mornings in "West End", the section of Atlanta in which Harris lived, when people would make an effort to catch the same street car that took him to town. They liked to catch "Joe Harris's Car" to hear his amusing sallies.

The people at Eatonton have a legend about their famous son's *one* public speech. At one time in that little town the people thought they had him cornered. He was on the platform with Henry Grady, and when the humorist's turn came the people called: "Harris! Harris!" "I'm coming," he answered, and walked down among the people and was lost in the crowd, escaping while the people laughed and cheered.

In a letter to his son, he once wrote, "Humor is a great thing to live by, and other things being equal, it is a profitable thing to die by." He seemed to have followed his own instruction;—a few days before his death, in answer to his son's inquiry as to how he felt, he replied, "I am about the extent of a tenth of a gnat's eyebrow better." But, as Julia Harris said of him, he knew the proper limits of humor:

No human being loved fun, frolic, folk-humor and droll buffoonery more than the creator of Billy Sanders, Uncle Remus, Brer Rabbit, Little Mr. Thimblefinger, and Mis' Meadows and de gals. On the other hand, no one more thoroughly disliked tawdry and filthy travesties of humor than did he. Happily he was spared the regret of seeing the negro's rich talent for mimicry, song and dance, which he had so skilfully and zestfully indicated in his pages, debased and burlesqued as it often is, today, on the stage or the screen or in the night-club.[25]

In addition to early indications of humor which were preparatory for the writing of the Uncle Remus stories, Harris had been experimenting in writing dialect, the medium through which the stories were related.

The first of Harris's songs written in dialect was "Revival Hymn" which appeared in *The Atlanta Constitution,* January 18, 1877. The first stanza of the hymn was:

Oh, whar shill we go w'en de great day comes,
Wid de blowin' er de trumpits en' de bangin' er de drums?
How many po' sinners 'll be kotched out late
En fine no latch ter de golden gate
  No use fer ter wait twel ter-morrer!
  De sun musn't set on yo' sorrer,
  Sin's ez sharp ez a bamboo-brier—
  Oh, Lord! fetch de mo'ners up higher!

The poem became popular throughout the State and was copied by many other newspapers. In November, 1877 there was printed in the "Editor's Drawer" of *Harper's Monthly,* a mangled version of Harris's original song. It was said to have been the product of a person of Ilion, New York. The following lines introduced the Ilion version: "From Ilion, New York where they make so many guns, comes this camp-meeting hymn of our colored brethren." The second line of the Ilion version was:

"Wid de blowin of de *trumps* and de banging of de *guns.*" Even a casual observer of the two versions could note the inaccuracy of the dialect of the Ilion version. *The*

Atlanta Constitution commented upon the theft and the changes from the original:

> It will be noted that in Ilion "Uncle Remus" has been re-inoculated with Fourth-of-July enthusiasm and has been made to predict the opening of Judgment Day with "de banging of de *guns*"—a sort of national salute to Gabriel and his "*trumps*", of which he will have a full hand, as we well know.[26]

Harris also contributed other songs in dialect to the *Constitution.*

By 1878, then, Joel Chandler Harris had established a reputation as a humorist and a writer of dialect. During the year, 1878, came the opportunity for the Uncle Remus stories upon which his fame now rests. Sam W. Small had been conducting in *The Atlanta Constitution* a column of anecdotes in which a Negro character, "Uncle Si", figured. When the newspaper changed hands, Mr. Small withdrew from the paper; and Captain Howell asked Harris if he could not carry on the series. "This," writes Julia Collier Harris, "father was not inclined to do, but he agreed to furnish something in another line. Uncle Remus's songs, sayings and fables was the result."[27]

There is remote possibility that Uncle Remus would have flourished and died within the columns of *The Atlanta Constitution* if Jefferson Davis had not signed a contract with D. Appleton & Co. to write a book on *The Rise and Fall of the Confederate Government.* The contract had been entered into in 1875: the manuscript was to be delivered within two years; but 1879 came to a close, and the manuscript had not been placed in Appleton's hands. Accordingly, J. C. Derby, as the Appleton's representative, went to visit Davis at the latter's home, Beauvoir, Mississippi. Davis had turned his documents over to a third party who was to prepare the manuscript for publication, and the third party had simply soldiered on the job. Matters were quickly adjusted, and the book appeared in 1881.

On his way back from Beauvoir, in February, 1880, Derby stopped in Atlanta and visited Harris with whom he had already been in correspondence, and arrangements were completed for the publication of *Uncle Remus: His Songs and His Sayings.*

II

FOLKLORE AND LITERARY ART

AMERICAN FOLKLORE BEGAN WITH UNCLE REMUS, some literary historians declare. Although one may not be able to accept so sweeping a verdict, for in a sense Franklin and Irving were folklorists, the claim for Harris is authentic enough to afford a convenient introduction to this section of the discussion. It is true that Harris's Tar-Baby story, published in *The Atlanta Constitution* in 1879 and widely read, antedates the organization of the American Folklore Society by nine years. It is true that Joel Chandler Harris was a charter member of the Society when it was founded. Furthermore, the first president of the Society stated in the first issue of its journal: ". . . . to Joel Chandler Harris belongs the credit for introducing to the public the type of story known as the 'Uncle Remus' story."

For at least a decade Harris's voice, nationally and internationally, was one of the most arresting. It seems safe to speculate that the Uncle Remus stories, published in 1880, if not the first of this distinctive type of literature, were at least prominently the means of creating a vogue which swept the country in the early 1880's. Pattee says:

"With the success of the first 'Uncle Remus' book, there came the greatest flood of dialect literature that America has ever known. The years 1883 and 1884 mark the high tide of this peculiar outbreak, and to Georgia more than any other locality may be traced the primal cause."[1]

Harris called himself "an accidental author"; his surprise at the flood of inquiries which came to him mark him as also "an accidental folklorist." The numerous letters which he received with regard to this element in his stories first amazed, then amused, but finally aroused and interested him. The Uncle Remus stories we know from his own statement were not written as folklore. To answer the correspondence with regard to the folklore element he had no more knowledge than "the man in the moon". He says:

> To be frank, I did not know much about folk-lore, and I didn't think that anybody else did. Imagine my surprise when I began to receive letters from learned philologists and folk-lore students from England to India, asking all sorts of questions and calling upon me to explain how certain stories told in the ricefields of India and on the cotton-fields of Georgia were identical, or similar, or at least akin. Then they wanted to know why this folk-lore had been handed down for centuries and perhaps for thousands of years. They wanted to know, too, why the negro makes Brer Rabbit so cunning and masterful. These letters came from royal institutes and literary societies, from scholars and from travelers. What answer could I make to them? None—none whatever. All that I know—all that we Southerners know—about it, is that every old plantation mammy in the South is full of these stories. One thing is certain—the negroes did not get them from the whites: probably they are of remote African origin.[2]

By December 8, 1880, the first Uncle Remus book had passed through the fourth edition. It had been noticed in every paper of importance in the country. Scientific journals devoted columns to it as a contribution to folklore. The stress laid upon this aspect of the stories sometimes annoyed Harris. He had occasion to write a review of some folk tales of the Southwest, and in this connection, he said: "First, let us have the folk-tales told as they were intended to be told, for the sake of amusement—as a part of the art of literary entertainment. Then, if the folk-lorists find in them anything of value to their pretensions let it be picked out and preserved with as little cackling as possible."[3]

With respect to the effect of the folklore interest upon him, Julia Harris comments:

> The aftermath of the appearance of "Uncle Remus: His Songs and His Sayings", demonstrated to father with peculiar force, one thing: that he was to be educated in the subject of folk-lore whether he willed it or not! I am certain that when " Uncle Remus" received his first greeting from the English-speaking public, his creator was ignorant of the fact that variants of the legend were to be found among so many of the primitive people.[4]

Again, she writes:

> Whether or not father had anything more than a passing interest in folk-lore *before* the stories were published, he certainly made some study of the subject later on. He was a subscriber to the "Folk-Lore Journal" published in London, and his library was well stocked with folk-lore of different nations; but never for one instant did the humorist and imaginative writer separate himself from his "bump of locality" and get lost in the complicated mazes of ethnic or philologic investigation . . . .[5]

Further evidence of his interest in the folklore aspect of the stories is furnished by a letter which he wrote to an Englishman in 1883, referring to one of the stories in *Uncle Remus: His Songs and His Sayings*. David Bogue brought out an English edition of the book in 1881. The name of the Englishman to whom the letter is written is not given.

Atlanta, Georgia, U.S.A.
1883: 28 June

Dear Sir:

A note from Mr. Brander Matthews informs me that you are interested in at least one of the Uncle Remus legends—the Crayfish and the Deluge. The history of that legend, as far as my knowledge of its genuineness extends, is this: I heard it told a number of times from 1862 to 1865 on the Turner Plantation (Putnam County—Middle Georgia) each time by a negro. The Remus legends, it should be said here, were not written with an eye to their importance as folk-lore stories. I had no more conception of that than the man in the moon. The first one was written out almost by accident, and as a study in dialect. It was so popular that I at once began to ransack my memory for others. My friends ransacked their memories, and the result was the book as it is printed—and another volume still to be printed, specimens of which you will find in the July "Century Magazine". But in order to make assurance doubly sure, I took the pains to verify every story anew, and, out of a variety of versions, to select the version that seemed to be most characteristic of the negro: so that it may be said that each legend comes fresh and direct from the negroes. My sole purpose in this was to preserve the stories dear to Southern children in the dialect of the cotton plantations.

To return: The crayfish story was told me by negroes on the Turner Plantation many times during the war period. It was recalled to me by a suggestion from the Editor of the "Savannah Daily News", who overheard it on the coast, and by other friends, and I then searched for it until I found it among the negroes of this—the Northern—section of the state. Since the publication of the book I have found a variant in which the Mud Turtle is substituted for the Crayfish.

I enclose with this a letter written some weeks ago to Mr. Laurence Gomme. I had decided not to post it for fear that the gentleman might be disposed to regard it as a presumptuous effort to intrude the Remus book upon his attention—notwithstanding the fact that my relation to the stories is that of compiler merely. Pray consider the letter as a postscript to this.

I shall be glad to give you any information you may desire in regard to the negro legends, or to serve you in any way, not merely because I am interested in the study of comparative folk-lore, but because the enjoyment I have obtained from some of your poems has made me your debtor.

Very truly yours
Joel Chandler Harris

The Constitution, Atlanta, Ga.
Editorial Rooms
Atlanta, Georgia, United States
9 June, 1883

Dear Sir:—

I have just been reading in the "Folk-Lore Journal" "The Hare in Folk-Lore", by William George Black, F.S.A., and his treatment of the subject has suggested to me the propriety of calling your attention to my little book "Uncle Remus and his Legends of the Old Plantation." (London: David Bogue, 1881.)

It is a misfortune, perhaps, from an English point of view, that the stories in that volume are rendered in the American negro dialect, but it was my desire to preserve the stories as far as I might be able, in the form in which I heard them, and to preserve also if possible, the quaint humor of the negro. It is his humor that gives the collection its popularity in the United States, but I think you will find the stories more important than humorous should you take the trouble to examine them. Not one of them is cooked, and not one nor any part of one is an invention of mine. They are all genuine folk-lore tales.

Since the publication of that book, I have interested myself in the matter, and, with the assistance of friends and correspondents in various parts of the Southern states, I have been enabled to gather seventy or eighty new ones. Pardon this letter. I am interested in the negro stories only as their compiler.

Very truly yours
Joel Chandler Harris

G. Laurence Gomme, F.S.A.
Editor Folk-lore Journal, London.[6]

After Harris's interest had been aroused in the folklore element of his stories, he persistently held that the stories were "uncooked"—that they were "pure folk-lore". The stories which appeared in the first book bear greater evidence of pure folklore than those which appeared in subsequent books. Perhaps the most convincing evidence that is offered in proof of the folklore element throughout the series is the inclusion in many of the stories of "Miss Meadows an' de gals". Of this subtle, whimsical creation —so intimately a part of the stories and existing in natural relationship with the animal creatures—Harris seems to have had no definite conception. In the story called "Mr. Rabbit Grossly Deceives Mr. Fox" the Little Boy asks Uncle Remus, "Who was Miss Meadows?" Uncle Remus replies: "Don't ax me, honey. She wuz in de tale, Miss Meadows en de gals wuz, en de tale I give you like hi't wer' gun ter me."[7] It seemed as if that was intended to end the inquiry.

The illustrations for the first edition of *Uncle Remus: His Songs and His Sayings* were to be done by Frederick Church and James Moser. Mr. Church's job was the delineation of the animals. Puzzled as to what he should do with "Miss Meadows an' de gals", he wrote Harris: "What is your idea of 'Miss Meadows an' de gals'? . . . perhaps they mean just *Nature*, in which case I should depict them as pretty girls in simple costumes, making a charming contrast to the ludicrous positions of the animals." [8]

Mr. Harris seemed pleased with the suggestion, but re-emphasized the idea that he was merely the "compiler" of the stories. He replied:

The Constitution, Atlanta, Ga.
Editorial Rooms, June 11, 1880

My Dear Mr. Church:—

My relations toward the sketches you are illustrating are those of compiler merely; consequently I cannot pretend to know what is meant by Miss Meadows. She plays a minor part in the entire series, as you will perceive when the concluding numbers have been sent you. Why she is there, I cannot say, but your conception will give to the sketches a poetical color (if I may say so) which will add vastly to whatever interest they may have for people of taste. By all means let Miss Meadows figure as Nature in the shape of a beautiful girl in a simple but not unpicturesque costume. As it is your own conception, I know you will treat the young lady tenderly . . . .

Yours very truly

J. C. Harris [9]

Kipling's curiosity was similarly aroused. Harris had written an appreciation of Kipling's *Jungle Book;* at the conclusion of a letter of appreciation dated December 6, 1895, which Kipling sent Harris, he said: "One thing I want to know badly (you must loathe the people who pester you with this kind of thing), but from what nature-myth or *what* come 'Miss Meadows and the girls?' Where did they begin—in whose mind? what do you think they are?"[10]

An examination of the Introductions to the first three volumes of the Uncle Remus stories (*Songs and Sayings,* 1880; *Nights,* 1883; *Friends,* 1892) is enlightening with regard to Harris's developing and then apparently waning interest in the folklore element. Evidently Harris had received many letters with regard to the folklore in stories which had appeared in newspapers and magazines prior to 1880. In the Introduction to the first book he refers to the correspondence and tells his amazement at the interest manifested in this particular phase of the tales. It is significant that the Uncle Remus sketches began appearing in the columns of *The Atlanta Constitution* as early as 1878, and that the Tar-Baby story (which was extremely popular at home and abroad) appeared in 1879. In the Introduction to the first book he tells of his method of collecting, of variants of the stories included in the volume, and insists that his aim is to preserve the stories in their "original simplicity." A portion of this Introduction is sufficiently important to be given in Harris's own words:

With respect to the Folk-Lore series, my purpose has been to preserve the legends themselves in their original simplicity, and to wed them permanently to the quaint dialect—if, indeed, it can be called a dialect—through the medium of which they have become a part of the domestic history of every Southern family; and I have endeavored to give the whole a genuine flavor of the old plantation.

Each legend has its variants, but in every instance I have retained that particular version which seemed to me to be the most characteristic, and have given it without embellishment and without exaggeration. The dialect, it will be observed, is wholly different from that of the Hon. Pompey Smash and his literary descendants, and different also from the intolerable misrepresentations of the ministrel stage, but it is at least phonetically genuine. Nevertheless, if the language of Uncle Remus fails to give vivid hints of the really poetic imagination of the negro; if it fails to embody the quaint and homely humor which was his most prominent characteristic; if it does not suggest a certain picturesque sensitiveness—a curious exaltation of mind and temperament not to be defined by words—then I have reproduced the form of the dialect merely, and not the essence, and my attempt may be accounted a failure. At any rate, I trust that I have been successful in presenting what must be, at least to a large portion of American readers, a new and by no means unattractive phase of negro character . . . .

A number of the plantation legends originally appeared in the columns of a daily newspaper—The Atlanta Constitution—and in that shape they attracted the attention of various gentlemen who were kind enough to suggest that they would prove to be valuable contributions to myth-literature. It is but fair to say that ethnological considerations formed no part of the undertaking which has resulted in the publication of this volume. Professor J. W. Powell, of the Smithsonian Institution, who is engaged in an investigation of the mythology of the North American Indians, informs me that some of Uncle Remus's stories appear in a number of different languages, and in various modified forms, among the Indians; and he is of the opinion that they are borrowed by the negroes from the red-men. But this, to say the least, is extremely doubtful.[11]

In 1870, Professor C. F. Hartt of Cornell University [12] heard at Santaren, on the Amazon, a story in *lingua geral* of "The Tortoise that Outran the Deer", a version of which he afterwards published in the *Cornell Era*

(January 20, 1871) and which attracted the attention of a writer in *The Nation* (February 23, 1871) who gave a variant of the same myth as found among the Negroes of South Carolina. Harris tells the same story in S. *and* S., "Mr. Rabbit Finds His Match at Last".

The curious resemblance between the Amazonian story told by Professor Hartt and the one found among the Negroes of South Carolina, a version of which Harris recounted was not noticed again until Mr. Herbert Smith, in his *Brazil, the Amazons and the Costa* (1879) in a chapter on "The Myths of the Amazonian Indians" gave a number of animal fables, merely noting the resemblances which had already attracted the attention of Professor Hartt and others. The proof-sheets of this chapter were sent to Mr. Harris, who at once saw that almost every story quoted by Mr. Smith had a parallel among the stories of the Southern Negroes, and some were so nearly identical in his opinion to point unmistakably to a common origin. Puzzled, Mr. Harris asks: "When did the negro or the North American Indian ever come in contact with the tribes of South America?"[13]

The tales in the first book, published in 1880, had delighted so large a circle that there was a growing demand for more stories. In October of 1882, Harris had been in correspondence with Mr. Osgood of the firm of Boston publishers regarding a second book. It seems that to supply the demand, Harris had sought the aid of a former newspaper associate, Mr. R. W. Grubb of Darien, a Georgia coast town.[14]

3 February, 1883

Dear Grubbs:—

Isn't there some one connected with your office who would be willing to piroot around among the negroes of Darien and gather me the outlines of the animal and alligator stories that form the basis of African mythology? I have a whole raft of stories current among the cotton plantation negroes, but there is another whole raft current among the coast negroes. Can't you get some one, who has the knack, to get in with some old negro, male or female, and secure me a dozen or more specimens? There are a number of stories in which the alligator figures, which I would like to have. All I want is a reasonably intelligent outline of the story as the Negroes tell them, and for such outlines I would be glad to pay what the collector may consider reasonable and fair. The only way to get at these stories is for the person seeking them to obtain a footing by telling one or two on his own hook—beginning, for instance, with the tar-baby. There are few negroes that will fail to respond to this.[15]

As a result of this letter, Mr. Grubb introduced Harris to Mrs. Helen Barclay who had gathered many stories on the Pierce Butler estates in the neighborhood of Darien. Others from whom Mr. Harris obtained outlines of tales were Mr. Charles C. Jones, who later compiled some of the stories he had heard into a book,[16] and Mr. John Devereux, who had been living in North Carolina. Mr. Devereux wrote: "I had been familiar with these stories from childhood and I sent Mr. Harris the bare outlines of several leaving it to his genius to make 'these dry bones live.' "[17]

In Harris's second book, *Nights with Uncle Remus,* (1883) the new type of interest both in the folk-lore element and the method of collecting is indicated in the prefatory material. In the earlier book, the author devotes eight pages of the Introduction to the discussion of this question; in the second book, he devotes twenty-nine pages to this aspect. He gives details about methods of collecting, comparative studies with Kaffir folk-tales, parallels of the Remus stories and Amazonian myths, similarities among Negro plantation proverbs and Kaffir proverbs, and a comparative study of the stories in his book with a volume of Negro stories of South Africa, translated by W. H. I. Bleek.[18] He also includes a dialect vocabulary, and the reprint of a French story, which brings out the Creole's use of dialect and the explanation that the Miss Meadows of the Georgia negro is Mamzel

Calinda of the Creoles.[19] He was "folk-lore conscious" to the extent that he wrote his publishers "I think I shall come to Boston to write the introduction, so as to take advantage of the folk-lore collection in the Harvard library. . . ."[20]

A detailed examination of some of the changes is enlightening: for instance, in the Introduction to the first book, he says very little about methods of collecting. Only a few lines are required to express his views on this subject: "Curiously enough, I have found few negroes who will acknowledge to a stranger that they know anything of these legends; and yet to relate one is the surest road to their confidence and esteem. In this way, and in this way only, have I been able to identify the folk-lore included in this volume."[21]

In the Introduction to the second book, *Nights with Uncle Remus,* he remarks that the thirty-four legends in the first volume were easy to verify because they were the most popular among the Negroes and were easily remembered, but many of the stories in the second volume were known only to a small group "who have the gift of story-telling,—a gift that is as rare among the blacks as among the whites."[22]

From the folklore point of view, he realized that the importance of the stories depended upon their verification, therefore, he let no opportunity pass that would aid him in the authentication. In the first book he had spoken of the diffidence of Negroes in releasing the stories; in the next book he relates in detail one instance in which he was successful in gaining the confidence of a group which was extremely valuable in verifying the legends. He wrote:

> One of these opportunities occurred in the summer of 1882, at Norcross, a little railroad station, twenty miles northeast of Atlanta. The writer was waiting to take the train to Atlanta, and this train, as it fortunately happened, was delayed. At the station were a number of negroes, who had been engaged in working on the railroad.

It was night, and, with nothing better to do, they were waiting to see the train go by. Some were sitting in little groups up and down the platform of the station, and some were perched upon a pile of cross-ties. They seemed to be in great good-humor, and cracked jokes at each other's expense in the midst of boisterous shouts of laughter. The writer sat next to one of the liveliest talkers in the party; and, after listening and laughing awhile, told the "Tar Baby" story by way of a feeler, the excuse being that some one in the crowd mentioned "Ole Molly Har' ". The story was told in a low tone, as if to avoid attracting attention, but the comments of the negro, who was a little past middle age, were loud and frequent. "Dar now!" he would exclaim, or, "He's a honey, mon!" or "Gentermen! git out de way, an' gin 'im room!" [23]

This brought the other Negroes near and they began to listen attentively. Harris next told the story of "Brer Rabbit and the Mosquitoes", with all the accompanying gestures. The group was so delighted that all began telling stories and for almost two hours a crowd of thirty or more vied with each other to see which could tell the most and best tales. Among the stories, Harris recognized many that he had already heard; a few were new. Thus, the stories included in the volume, *Nights with Uncle Remus,* embody legends heard by the author supplemented by those collected by his friends. Furthermore, they were rendered more with an eye to their ethnological importance.

Nine years elapsed between the printing of *Nights With Uncle Remus* and the appearance of *Uncle Remus and His Friends,* (1892). During these years, Harris's interest in the folklore element seems to have waned. As for the collecting of the stories for this volume, he seemed to have relied primarily upon two sources. In the Introduction to this volume, he wrote:

The stories here gathered have been caught for me in the kitchen. Some of them are discoveries, many are verifications of stories that have been sent me by friends, and others are the odds and ends and fragments from my notebooks which I have been able to verify and complete. This work of verification and putting together has been going on since 1884, but not in any definite or systematic way. There has been a general understanding in my household for a dozen years or more that preference was to be given in the kitchen to a cook of the plantation type,—the type that we have come to call here the "old-timey" negro. Naturally, it has sometimes happened that digestion was sacrificed to sentiment, but the special result is to be found in the pages that follow.[24]

The other source for the fathering of these stories was also a "home source"; namely, his children. He states that there was a general agreement that the children should use all their arts to discover a new story or to verify one already in hand. The plan was to give the children a cue word or phrase from a story that needed verification or from an interesting fragment that lacked completion. Harris relates one particular instance in which this plan had excellent results. His rehearsal of it is worth noting:

The cook in charge had a son-in-law named John Holder, who had shown a tendency to indulge in story-telling in his hours of ease. This was in 1886. Mr. Richard Adams Learned of Newton, Sussex County, New Jersey, had sent me the story about the man who, with his two dogs, harassed the wild cattle. (See p. 91). One of the youngsters was told to ask about this story, and his cue was "a man, two dogs, and the wild cattle".[25] But the child's memory was short. He asked about a boy and two dogs, and the result was the story of "The Little Boy and his Dogs", to be found in the supplementary part of "Daddy Jake, the Runaway" (page 76). Some months afterwards the child remembered the wild cattle, and got the story from John Holder substantially as it had been sent me by Mr. Learned. The variations are not worth taking into account. I have referred to this matter because it has been made interesting by an article which Mr. David Dwight Wells contributes to the "Popular Science Monthly", for May, 1892. Mr. Wells embodies the wild cattle story, which differs in no essential particular from the version sent me by Mr. Learned. Mr. Wells had the story from a gentleman who was born about the beginning of this century in Essequibo, British Guiana, South America. The story was told to Mr. Learned by his grandfather (born in 1802), who had it from his old "mammy" nurse in Demarara. In John Holder's story the names of the dogs are changed to Minny-minny-morack and Follamalinska; in Mr. Learned's story the names are Yarmeàroo and Gengamoroto, in Mr. Wells's, Ya-me-o-ro and Cen-ga-mo-ro-to. The Georgia negro had the story pat, and out of it grew the tale of the "Bull that went a-courting . . ." which the wild cattle story seems to be the sequel of. Thus, we have a series that ought to be of some interest to students of folk-lore.[26]

However, he hastens to add that he is unable to handle the folklore branch of the subject. In fact, he devotes but three pages to the discussion of this element in the book as compared to eight pages in the first volume and twenty-nine in the second. He seems definitely convinced that he knows less now about folklore than he has ever known. He says:

But the folk-lore branch of the subject I gladly leave to those who think they know something about it. My own utter ignorance I confess without a pang. To know that you are ignorant is a valuable form of knowledge, and I am gradually accumulating a vast store of it. In the light of this knowledge, the enterprising inconsequence of the Introduction to "Nights with Uncle Remus" is worth noting on account of its unconscious and harmless humor. I knew a good deal more about comparative folk-lore then than I know now; and the whole affair is carried off with remarkable gravity. Since that Introduction was written, I have gone far enough into the subject (by the aid of those who are Fellows of This and Professors of That, to say nothing of Doctors of the Other) to discover that at the end of investigation and discussion Speculation stands grinning.[27]

We may presume that Harris was also "grinning" at many of the folklorists and their deductions. An excerpt from a letter published in the *Critic* in September, 1882, regarding a collection of American Indian myths reveals that Harris regarded lightly his reputation in the field of folklore:

I am not specially well versed in folk-lore, but I presume this collection will possess scientific value. . . . It would be a wonder if any contribution to myth-literature could be made that would not be promptly traced, historically or psychologically, to the Aryan sun-myth—as, for instance, if a South American cotia creeps in at one end of a hollow log and out at the other, or if Brer Fox runs Brer Rabbit into a hollow tree, we have the going down and the rising of the sun typified. And really the sun-myth does nobody any harm; if it is quackery it is quackery of a very mild kind.[28]

Not only did he treat lightly his reputation as a folklorist, but he also discounted the literary value of his productions and his own art of re-telling. In a letter to William Baskervill, dated March 18, 1895, he wrote:

I have tried to keep Joel Chandler Harris as much out of my work as possible and I think I have succeeded in the sense that so many others have failed—that is to say, what I have written was for its own sake, and not for money nor for the glorification of the man who was accidentally behind it all. And yet the man is there somewhere—standing for lack of cultivation, lack of literary art, and lack of all the graces that make life worth living to those who affect culture; but I hope that honesty, sincerity, and simplicity are not lacking. . . . I should be delighted to see you seize hold of the manifold defects in my stuff, deal with them generously but candidly, and so point out to the younger writers that all this talk, this silly chatter, of making a literary reputation in an hour is nonsense. I have tried hard to get at the secret of literary art, and have failed. I have had the knack of hard work, but the gift has somehow been lacking.

Nobody knows better than I do how far below the level of permanence my writings fall. . . .[29]

In his Introduction to *Gabriel Tolliver,* he further enlarged upon the absence of any "idea of art" in his writings:

Let those who can do so continue to import harmony and unity into their fabrications and call it art. Whether it be art or artificiality, the trick is beyond my powers. I can only deal with things as they were; on many occasions they were far from what I would have had them be; but as I was powerless to change them, so I am powerless to twist individuals and events to suit the demands or necessities of what is called art.[30]

Of the Uncle Remus stories he said:

But there is no pretense that the . . . poor little stories are in the nature of literature, or that their re-telling touches literary art at any point. All the accessories are lacking. There is nothing here but an old negro man, a little boy, and a dull reporter, the matter of discourse being fantasies as uncouth as the original man ever conceived of.[31]

Despite the persistent refusal to acknowledge his art, Harris's correspondence and the productions themselves point to the fact that he did have skill, that he did, in some instances, consciously develop the art of writing through deliberate self-discipline. His awareness of the differentiating qualities of style and diction is noted in a letter to his daughter; in the same letter, he also sets forth the secrets of good writing.

May Day, Sunday, 1898

Dear Lillian:—

The Gleanings came to hand, and I read your account of the pottery tour with great pleasure. It is particularly well done, and the reason is very plain. You had something to write about, you knew what you wanted to say, and you said it, briefly and clearly. There are two secrets of good writing that I will whisper in your ear. One is to write about something that interests you because you know it; the other is to be familiar with and believe in the ideas you propose to write about. One secret refers to description, and the other to views, feelings, opinions. Combined, or separate, they relate to everything that has been or can be written in the shape of literature. So far as merely correct diction is concerned, that can easily be acquired, especially by those who have a knack or gift of expression.

In nearly all the books and magazines that I read, diction is called style. Why, I don't know, for the two come together and combine only in the works of the very greatest writers, as, for instance, Hawthorne—or, to name a greater still, Cardinal Newman. I have just been reading some of the Cardinal's works, and I am simply amazed at the beauty, power, fluency and vividness with which he uses the English tongue. In discussing the dryest subjects, he frequently thrills the mind with passages of such singular beauty as almost to take one's breath away. In these passages you cannot separate the style from the diction, for they are fused.

Nevertheless, style is one thing and diction is another. If some one should compel me by force to explain the difference between the two my answer would be something like this: Diction is the body—the flesh and bone—and style is the spirit. But some years ago, that able Heathen, Mr. Herbert Spencer, had something he wanted to say about diction, and so he wrote it out and called it An Essay on Style, and ever since then the Heathens, the Pagans, and not a few who call themselves Christians, have persisted in referring to diction as style—just as our Northern scholars refer to the "*provincialism* of the South," when they mean the *provinciality* of the South. Dear me! I hope I am not wearying you with all this; more than all, I hope I have made myself understood. It is so easy to be vague and hazy when talking about writing as a gift and as an art. A person who has the gift must acquire the art, and that is to be done only by long practice.[32]

Perhaps Joe Harris was not conscious of the ability of Joel Chandler Harris. He always insisted upon his dual personality. The letter which follows was written to his daughter; in this, he offers an explanation of himself as a writer:

As for myself—though you could hardly call me a real, sure enough author—I never have anything but the vaguest ideas of what I am going to write; but when I take my pen in my hand, the rust clears away and the "other fellow" takes charge. You know all of us have two entities, or personalities. That is the reason you see and hear persons "talking to themselves". They are talking to the "other fellow". I have often asked my "other fellow" where he gets all his information, and how he can remember, in the nick of time, things that I have forgotten long ago; but he never satisfies my curiosity. He is simply a spectator of my folly until I seize a pen, and then he comes forward and takes charge.

Sometimes I laugh heartily at what he writes. If you could see me at such times, and they are very frequent, you would no doubt say, "It is very conceited in that old man to laugh at his own writing." But that is the very point; it is not my writing at all; it is my "other fellow" doing the work and I am getting all the credit for it. Now, I'll admit that I write the editorials for the paper. The "other fellow" has nothing to do with them, and, so far as I am able to get his views on the subject, he regards them with scorn and contempt; though there are rare occasions when he helps me out on a Sunday editorial. He is a creature hard to understand, but, so far as I can understand him, he's a very sour, surly fellow until I give him an opportunity to guide my pen in subjects congenial to him; whereas, I am, as you know, jolly, good-natured, and entirely harmless.

Now, my "other fellow", I am convinced, would do some damage if I didn't give him an opportunity to work off his energy in the way he delights. I say to him, "Now, here's an editor who says he will pay well for a short story. He wants it at once." Then I forget all about the matter, and go on writing editorials and taking Celery Compound and presently my "other fellow" says sourly: "What about that story?" Then when night comes, I take up my pen, surrender unconditionally to my "other fellow", and out comes the story, and if it is a good story I am as much surprised as the people who read it. Now, my dear gals will think I am writing nonsense; but I am telling them the truth as near as I can get at the facts—for the "other fellow" is secretive.[33]

To discover Harris's art one has only to examine one of the "uncooked" stories as sent him by a Negro correspondent and compare it with the finished version. An exact report of a correspondent from Senoia, Georgia was:

Mr. Harris I have one tale of Uncle Remus that I have not seen in print yet. Bro Rabbit at Mis Meadows and Bro Bare went to Bro Rabbit house and eat up his childrun and set his house on fire and make like the childrun all burnt up but Bro Rabbit saw his track he knowed Bro Bare was the man so one day Bro Rabbit saw Bro Bare in the woods with his ax hunting a bee tree after Bro Rabbit spon howdy he tell Bro Bare he know whare a bee tree was and he would go an show and help him cut it down they went and cut it an Bro Rabbit drove in the glut [wedge] while Bro Bare push his head in the hole Bro Rabbit nock out the glut and cut him hickry. Mr. Harris you have the tale now give it wit I never had room to give you all you can finish it.[34]

This tale was the source of the story which appeared in *Uncle Remus: His Songs and His Sayings,* under the title "The End of Mr. Bear".[35] One has only to read the tale as given by Harris to recognize the craftsman's art. A comparison of the two versions proves that Harris was no mere copyist. Despite his stubborn insistence that the stories were "pure folklore", they seem "folklore somewhat embroidered."

One of the best appraisals in connection with the respective literary and folklore elements is that given by Mark Twain. On August 4, 1881, Harris had written in a letter to Mark Twain:

Everybody has been kind to the old man, but you have been kindest of all. I am perfectly aware that my book has no basis of literary art to stand upon; I know it is the matter and not the manner that has attracted public attention and won the consideration of people of taste at the North; I understand that my relations toward Uncle Remus are similar to those that exist between an almanac-maker and the calendar; but at the same time I feel grateful to those who have taken the old man under their wing.[36]

Mark Twain realized his friend's modest valuation of his talents, and in his reply stated:

You can argue *yourself* into the delusion that the principle of life is in the stories themselves and not in their setting, but you will save labor by stopping with that solitary convert, for he is the only intelligent one you will bag. In reality the stories are only alligator pears—one eats them merely for the sake of the dressing. "Uncle Remus" is most deftly drawn and is a lovable and delightful creation; he and the little boy and their relations with each other are bright, fine literature, and worthy to live. . . .[37]

2

ANALYSIS OF THE UNCLE REMUS BOOKS

". . . . de ol' times done gone, an' ef twa'nt fer deze ol' tales nobody wouldn't know dat dey y'ever wuz any ol' times."

—*Uncle Remus Returns.*

III

GENERAL DESCRIPTION OF THE UNCLE REMUS BOOKS

"Well, 'tain't ez you may say one er deze yer reg'lar up en down tales, what runs crossways. Dish yer tale goes straight."—Uncle Remus and His Friends.

THE UNCLE REMUS STORIES CAME TO THE WORLD AS A novelty—a genre not readily classifiable—a curious salmagundi of folklore, of picturesque locale, of humor (frequently bordering on pathos), of vital characterization, of spicy wit and quaint dialect. To the North, they were a revelation of the unknown; to the South, they were an eye-opener to the charm of the familiar.

To most Americans, the chief ingredient was humor. It was a new kind of humor in the history of American literature. Coming from a race good natured in the face of affliction, there was in it a propinquity of smiling and weeping, a wit which grew out of the fact that the ability to make an owner smile often saved a harsh lash. The odd quips and quiddities, the satirical and philosophical turns of thought, were heightened by the use of dialect—the best representation which has yet been given. Though humorous, Harris's portrayal seems genuinely sympathetic. He wrote in the Introduction to his first book:

> I am advised by my publishers that this book is to be included in their catalogue of humorous publications, and this friendly warning gives me an opportunity to say that however humorous it may be in effect, its intention is perfectly serious; and, even if it were otherwise, it seems to me that a volume written wholly in dialect must have its solemn, not to say melancholy, features.[1]

Other elements there were, outstanding among which was characterization—and characterization here means chiefly the creation of Uncle Remus. Harris once said, "What does a story matter, if we do not, somehow, find its characters close kin to us?"[2] Of the gift of characterization, he wrote:

> Can a writer properly portray the mental emotions, the aspirations as well as the inner habits of thought, of aliens and strangers of whom he has only a surface knowledge? . . . This is a question that goes to the very heart of successful fiction. A writer must not only have the knowledge of them, but he must know them to the very root of their being. Only in this way can character be created, and the creation of character is the chief end and aim of those who set themselves to produce masterpieces of fiction.[3]

And again:

> Wherever, or whenever, you find a book the apt and happy portrayal of *human nature,* its contests with its own emotions and temptations, its striving toward the highest ideals, its passions, its platitudes, its meanness, its native longing for what is true and wholesome, its struggles with circumstances, its surrenders and its victories, and, above all, its *humor,* there you will find the passport and credentials that will commend it to readers yet unborn.[4]

A more detailed discussion of Harris's power of characterization will be given in later pages. It remains to be said here that the success of the first Uncle Remus book was instantaneous, but that when one seeks to find the secret of that success, it seems to be in no one merit.

Perhaps there was nothing unique about what Harris did; maybe it was the combination of many things, or the innovation of a few things which caught the public eye and held it. In the series of Uncle Remus books three elements deserve consideration: the pattern, the characters, and the chronological order of volumes.

PATTERN

The pattern was an innovation recognized by all readers of stories. Though Harris said, "There is nothing here but an old negro man, a little boy, and a dull reporter", yet one realizes that this strong frame in which his portraits were placed was an artistic conception. In the Introduction to the first book, Harris acquaints the reader with the setting:

> If the reader not familiar with plantation life will imagine that the myth-stories of Uncle Remus are told night after night to a little boy by an old negro who appears to be venerable enough to have lived during the period which he describes—who has nothing but pleasant memories of the discipline of slavery—and who has all the prejudices of caste and pride of family that were the natural results of the system; if the reader can imagine all this, he will find little difficulty in appreciating and sympathizing with the air of affectionate superiority which Uncle Remus assumes as he proceeds to unfold the mysteries of plantation lore to a little child who is the product of that practical reconstruction which has been going on to some extent since the war in spite of the politicians.[5]

He opens the Uncle Remus series by presenting this pair whom one meets in every book:

> One evening recently, the lady whom Uncle Remus calls "Miss Sally" missed her little seven-year-old boy. Making search for him through the house and through the yard, she heard the sound of voices in the old man's cabin, and, looking through the window, saw the child sitting by Uncle Remus. His head rested against the old man's arm, and he was gazing with an expression of the most intense interest into the rough, weather-beaten face, that beamed so kindly upon him.[6]

Again he describes them:

> . . . . the two—old age and youth, one living in the Past and the other looking forward only to the Future—gazed into the bed of glowing embers illuminated by a thin, flickering flame. Probably they saw nothing there, each being busy with his own simple thoughts; but their shadows, enlarged out of all proportion, and looking over their shoulders from the wall behind them, must have seen something, for, clinging together, they kept up a most incessant pantomime. . . . The sorrows and perplexities of nearly a hundred years lay between them; and now, as always, the baffled eyes of age gazed into the Sphinx-like face of youth, as if by this means to unravel the mysteries of the past and solve the problems of the future.[7]

The picture of the old man and a little boy is the same in nine of the books. However, in *Nights with Uncle Remus,* though the frame remains the same, the portrait is enlarged by the addition of three other characters who appear in roles of both narrators and auditors. The additional characters are 'Tildy, Daddy Jack, and Aunt Tempy.

There are seventy-one stories included in *Nights.* Daddy Jack is introduced in Story XXV, and remains either as narrator or auditor intermittently throughout the series. Harris probably had several motives for the introduction of this character: first, Daddy Jack came from the coast, and it was generally presumed that the coastal Negroes were more superstitious than those of the inland counties; second, Daddy Jack spoke the "Gullah" dialect, and his presence provided an opportunity to contrast the dialect which he spoke with that of the group of Middle Georgia. Further, Harris's skill is evident here in showing that the stories were true folklore because a story told by Uncle Remus or Aunt Tempy would frequently remind Daddy Jack of a similar one he had heard. Though basically the same story, he would preface his variant by saying: "Oona no bin-a yerry um lak me." (You haven't heard it like me.)

Daddy Jack relates but five of the stories in the series, several of which have to do with ghosts or conjury, but his presence gives the necessary atmosphere for the relation of other stories which deal with similar topics. Finally, there is the episode of Daddy Jack's and 'Tildy's violent love affair—first, her rejection of his proposal of marriage, and her final acceptance and marriage—an episode which forms the central theme of the last story in the series, "The Night Before Christmas." The book ends with a song, "My Honey, My Love," which was sung at the marriage celebration.

As for the other narrators, Aunt Tempy tells five stories and 'Tildy, two. A final reason for the change of story-teller might be to show, by contrast, Uncle Remus as a past master in the art. Certainly he is the one who compels and lingers; the others one quickly forgets.

Another change in the accustomed pattern occurs (also in *Nights*); this is the introduction of Miss Motts to the group of "Miss Meadows en' de gals". Uncle Remus says: " . . . de creeturs wuz constant gwine a-courtin'. Ef twan't Miss Meadows en de gals, de wuz flyin' 'roun', hit uz Miss Motts." Miss Motts recurs in a few stories, but she remains as shadowy a character as Miss Meadows.

CHARACTERS

UNCLE REMUS—Uncle Remus calls for special emphasis. Harris retires behind the scene and allows the wise, genial old man not only to tell the stories but also to express psychological and philosophical reactions to the world in which he lives. Upon the inquiry of an interviewer as to who suggested the character, Harris replied that he was not an invention of his own but a human syndicate of three or four old negroes whom he had just "walloped together".[8]

Despite this remark by Harris, and the statements of most critics that Uncle Remus represents a whole race, what Harris gave to literature was not a Character but a Portrait. Uncle Remus was an individual—a distinctive personality. As Irvin S. Cobb has the hero of *J. Poindexter, Colored* say of himself, "I ain't no problem, I'se a pusson; I craves to be so regarded." Well might Uncle Remus say, "I ain't no race, I'se an individual; I craves to be so regarded." Harris's aim was not to give a picture of an entire race; what he did was to choose from that race a dramatic human figure that appealed to him as picturesque and moving. It is true that he used the plantation as the background against which the old man's figure was silhouetted, for Uncle Remus could not have existed independently of his setting. Yet, he was a genius in the art of story-telling—few there were in fiction or in real life who could reach his stature. Story-telling is an art and Uncle Remus was an artist.

Perhaps Pattee's statement concerning Uncle Remus best explains his status: "Harris embodied the results of his studies not in a type, but in a single negro personality to which he gave the breath of life. Harris's negro is the type plus the personal equation of an individual—Uncle Remus is one of the few original characters that America has added to the world gallery." [9]

Of Uncle Remus's physical appearance, Harris wrote:

> The figure of the old man, as he stood smiling upon the crowd of negroes, was picturesque in the extreme. He seemed to be taller than all the rest; and, not withstanding his venerable appearance, he moved and spoke with all the vigor of youth. He had always exercised authority over his fellow-servants. He had been the captain of the corn-pile, the stoutest at the log-rolling, the swiftest with the hoe, the neatest with the plough, and the plantation hands still looked upon him as their leader.[10]

Of his position on the plantation, we learn:

> Uncle Remus was not a "field hand"; that is to say, he was not required to plow and hoe and engage in the rough work on the plantation.
>
> It was his business to keep matters and things straight about the

house, and to drive the carriage when necessary. He was the confidential family servant, his attitude and his actions showing that he considered himself a partner in the various interests of the plantation. He did no great amount of work, but he was never wholly idle. He tanned leather, he made shoes, he manufactured horse-collars, fish-baskets, foot-mats, scouring-mops, and ax-handles for sale; he had his own watermelon-and cotton-patches; he fed the hogs, looked after the cows and sheep, and, in short, was the busiest person on the plantation.

He was reasonably vain of his importance, and the other negroes treated him with great consideration. They found it to their advantage to do so, for Uncle Remus was not without influence with his master and mistress. It would be difficult to describe, to the satisfaction of those not familiar with some of the developments of slavery in the South, the peculiar relations existing between Uncle Remus and his mistress, whom he called "Miss Sally." He had taken care of her when she was a child, and he still regarded her as a child.

He was dictatorial, overbearing, and quarrelsome. These words do not describe Uncle Remus's attitude, but no other words will do. Though he was dictatorial, overbearing and quarrelsome, he was not even grim. Beneath everything he said there was a current of respect and affection that was thoroughly understood and appreciated.[11]

In a letter to William Baskervill, Harris gives his conception of Uncle Remus as differing from his other characters:

Uncle Remus is a composite character. He plays many parts. But in my mind as he appears to the inner eye—he is more surely an individual than the majority of the people I meet. All my other characters are delineations—types—suggestions—experiments—but Uncle Remus alone is a development.[12]

Uncle Remus was not the first plantation story-teller in fiction;[13] but none had so completely revealed himself as did he. Herein lay the essence of Harris's art: one is convinced, after reading the ten books, of the careful and complete delineation of the man. Harris reveals Uncle Remus's method: "He liked to be asked for a story so that he might have an opportunity of indulging in a friendly dispute, a wrangle of words, and then suddenly end it all by telling the tale that happened to be on his mind at the moment. In short, he delighted to whet the expectations of the youngster, and arouse his enthusiasm." [14]

Harris uses the dramatic monologue as a principal means of character revelation, though brief descriptions of the old man interpolated throughout the stories add to the graphic presentation. The dramatic monologue was certainly no new form in literature, but Harris put it to new uses, aided by his unrivalled power of language and his accurate knowledge of folk speech. What makes Uncle Remus so true to life is that Harris captured not only what the man said, but his manner of saying it, his every gesture. To transfer these to the printed page was indeed a difficult art, but these are the touches that elevate Harris's character to originality, and establish for him the reputation as master in the art of creation of atmosphere and specifically the creation of a character who breathes. The old man is fond of pictorial instruction, much of which is found in conversation carried on with fidelity and naturalness. The venerable fabulist was apparently Harris's embodiment of the aim stated in the Introduction to his first book, " . . . to present the picturesque sensitiveness—a curious exaltation of mind and temperament, not to be defined by words."

Various are the roles which Uncle Remus plays. Sometimes he scourges mischief: "I boun' I ain't gwine ter fix you up no mo' contraptions, ef dat's de way you does—massycreein' de cats, en de Dominicker chickens, en de Lord knows what! Ef you er huntin' war, des go up yonder whar dat ar Dominicker hen got de young chickens; go up dar en 'sturb her, en ef she don't make you squall de first letter er my name ain't Remus." [15]

Uncle Remus's method of quarreling with the little boy was inimitable. The youngster had learned to be obedient if he wanted the story finished. For example:

"Well, honey," said the old man, wiping his spectacles, "hit sorter runs dis away: One time dey wuz a man w'at had a mighty likely daughter."

"Was he a white man or a black man?" the little boy asked.

"I 'clar' ter gracious, honey!" exclaimed the old man, "you er pushin' me mos' too close. Fer all I kin tell you, de man mount er bin ez w'ite ez de driven snow, er he mout er bin de blackes' Affi'kin er de whole kit en bilin'. I'm des tellin' you de tale, en you kin take en take de man en w'itewash 'im, er you kin black 'im up des ez you please. Dat's de way I looks at it." [16]

Or again:

"Now, den," Uncle Remus continued, settling himself more comfortably in his chair, "dish yer man wuz a witch."

"Why, I thought a witch was a woman," said the little boy.

The old man frowned and looked into the fire.

"Well, sir," he remarked with some emphasis, "ef you er gwine ter tu'n de man inter a 'oman, den dey won't be no tale, kaze dey's bleege ter be a man right dar whar I put dis un. Hit's des like I tole you 'bout de color er de man. Black 'im er whitewash 'im des es you please, en ef you want ter put a frock on 'im ter boot, hit ain't none er my business; but I'm gwine ter 'low he wuz a man ef it's de las' ac'."

The little boy remained silent, and Uncle Remus went on:

"Now, den, dish yer man was a witch. He could cunjer folks, mo' 'speshually dem folks w'at ain't got no rabbit foot." [17]

He disliked having his authority questioned.

In the story, "Mr. Fox Gets Into Serious Business," he states, "hit turn out one time dat Brer Rabbit make so free wid de man's collardpatch dat de man he tuck'n sot a trap fer old Brer Rabbit."

The little boy asked, "Which man was that, Uncle Remus?" "Des a man, honey. Dat's all. Dat's all I knows —des wunner dese yer mans w'at you see trollopin 'roun' eve'y day. Nobody ain't never year w'at his name is, en ef dey did dey kep' de news mighty close fum me. Ef dish yer man is bleedzd fer ter have a name, den I'm done, kaze you'll hatter go fudder dan me. . . ."

"Well, I just thought, Uncle Remus," said the little boy, in a tone remarkable for self-depreciation, "that the man had a name."

"Tooby sho," replied the old man, with unction, puffing away at his pipe. "Co'se. Dat w'at make I say w'at I duz. Dish yer man mout a had a name, en den ag'in he moutn't. He mout er bin name Slipshot Sam, en he mouter bin name ole One-eye Riley, w'ich ef 'twuz hit ain't bin handed roun' ter me. But dish yer man, he in de tale, en w'at we gwine do wid 'im? Dat's de p'int, kase w'en I git ter huntin' 'roun' 'mong my 'membunce atter dish yer Mister W'atyoumaycollum's name, she ain't dar. Now den, les des call 'im Mr. Man en let 'im go at dat."

The silence of the little boy gave consent.

At another time he cautions the little boy about his choice of friends: "I dunner w'at in der name er goodness you wanter be copyin' atter dem ar Favereses fer. Ef youer gwine ter copy atter yuther folks, copy atter dem w'at some 'count." [18] But no offense of the little boy is so great that it cannot be removed by the sight of "tater pie" or cookies. Moreover, Uncle Remus realizes his power as a storyteller; when the little boy misses him from the "big house", and goes to his cabin to inquire why he has not been to tell him a story, to his inquiry Uncle Remus replies, " . . . when de spoon want anything it hatter go ter de bowl."

Sometimes he is the philosopher. One day when he and the little boy are talking over things in general, he remarks:

'Tain't de biggest en de strongest dat does de mostest in dis world. . . . No honey, don't let nobody fool you 'bout dat. De cuckle-burr got needer life ner lim', yit when it gits in de sheep wool it kin travel fast ez de sheep, you know dat . . . de ole elephen' may be strong, en de tiger may be servigrous . . . but Brer Rabbit done outdone um.[19]

He is always engaged in some form of activity—oiling the harness, half-soling shoes, making a horse collar, grinding his axe; in the midst of these occupations he spins the tale, with which are mixed many other ingredients. He indulges in aphorisms, shrewd observations, curious retorts, homely thrusts—all of which become a commentary on life. Sometimes the criticism takes a pungent turn; often one notices a felicity of phrase abounding in similes and metaphors; frequently there is a poetic release where his words move with rhythm and flow with eloquence. There are passages which reveal an imagination which may come from the Celtic strain in Harris. Note how he describes old times, " . . . way back yander when de clouds wuz thicker dan what dey is now, an' when de sun ain't had ter go to bed at night ter keep fum being tired de next day."[20] He delighted in mouth-filling, many-syllabled words, some of which seem nonsensical, but appealed to him because of their sonority. Uncle Remus also talks of gossip, "De word went 'roun' an' when it come back ter whar it started, it ain't look like itse'f;" he knows something of the gossip-monger, "She had a tongue wid salt en pepper on it."

So distinct a personality as Uncle Remus may never again be chronicled. His naive drollery, his whimsical incongruities, his aphorisms, quaintly expressed—all peculiar to himself—make up his character. He caught them from no one and to no one has he imparted them.

THE LITTLE BOY

There are two Little Boys who appear in the series. The

one who listens to the stories in *Songs and Sayings, Nights,* and *Friends* is the child of "Miss Sally". He is an alert, eager, high-spirited lad, full of curiosity and fond of playing pranks. The Little Boy who listens to the stories in the subsequent book is the son of the first Little Boy. He is more like a girl in his refinement; all the boyishness has been taken out of him by that mysterious "course of discipline that some mothers know how to apply." He was so great a contrast to his father that Uncle Remus and Miss Sally, the grandmother, were alarmed about him. This particular Little Boy never appeared anxious for a story unless the old man led up to it by means of comment or conversation, or indicated it by some evasive illusion, and Uncle Remus doubted frequently whether the tale had been an enjoyable one, for the boy seldom laughed and "What the old man liked best of all things was to hear children laugh. . . . Most of his quarrels were mock quarrels and his severest frowns always had pretense for a basis."

Uncle Remus was a tradition in the family, and before the second Little Boy met him he felt as if he knew him:

> The little boy was as much interested in Uncle Remus himself as he was in the stories he told, for the old man had already developed into a tradition. His name was as much a part of the family as that of any member thereof—and if the child had any hero, such as dwell in the realm of mystery and romance, it was Uncle Remus himself, with his gray head and his air of belonging to some other place and some other time; and all this in spite of the fact that no other person could take his place or fit or fill the position which he occupied.[21]

'TILDY—the house girl plays an inconspicuous part. She is genial, full of fun, and enjoys tormenting Uncle Remus who is frequently quarreling with her.

The other two characters may be described in Harris's own words:

> DADDY JACK—Daddy Jack was an object of curiosity to older

people than the little boy. He was a genuine African, and for that reason he was known as African Jack, though the child had been taught to call him Daddy Jack. He was brought to Georgia in a slaveship when he was about twenty years old, and remained upon one of the sea-islands for several years. Finally, he fell into the hands of the family of which Uncle Remus's little partner was the youngest representative, and became the trusted foreman of a plantation in the Southern part of Georgia, known as Walthall Place. Once every year he was in the habit of visiting the Home Place in Middle Georgia, and it was during one of these annual visits that the little boy found him in Uncle Remus's cabin.

Daddy Jack appeared to be quite a hundred years old, but he was probably not more than eighty. He was a little, dried-up old man, whose weazened, dwarfish appearance, while it was calculated to inspire awe in the minds of the superstitious, was not without its pathetic suggestions. The child had been told that the old African was a wizard, a conjurer, and a snake-charmer; but he was not afraid, for in any event,— conjuration, witchcraft, or what not,— he was assured of the protection of Uncle Remus.[22]

AUNT TEMPY— . . . a woman of large authority on the place, who stood next to Uncle Remus in the confidence of her mistress. Aunt Tempy was a fat, middle-aged woman, who always wore a head-handkerchief, and kept her sleeves rolled up, displaying her plump arms. . . . She never hesitated to exercise her authority, and the younger negroes on the place regarded her as a tyrant; but in spite of her loud voice and brusque manners she was thoroughly good-natured, usually good-humored, and always trustworthy. Aunt Tempy and Uncle Remus were secretly jealous of each other, but they were careful never to come in conflict, and, to all appearances, the most cordial relations existed between them.[23]

MISS SALLY and MARSE JOHN— . . . are frequently present in the background. "Marse John" was a private in the Northern Army who was shot out of a tree by Uncle Remus as he was preparing to kill a Southerner. "Miss Sally" nursed the soldier to recovery and later married him.

Uncle Remus's disputes with "Miss Sally" were always amusing to "Marse John" who, when appealed to, generally made a decision favorably to Uncle Remus. All his quarrels with his mistress were about trifles, his dictatorial bearing was inconsequential, and she frequently made remarks that she knew would bring an argument from the old man.

THE CHRONOLOGICAL ORDER OF VOLUMES

The first Uncle Remus book was published in 1880, though the title page gives the year 1881. This contains thirty-four legends of the old plantation, which comprise 162 pages of the 273. The other sections include four pages of plantation proverbs, a story of the war, nine songs, and twenty-one sayings. (The sayings are really incidents in the life of Uncle Remus.) The 1880 edition was illustrated by F. S. Church and J. H. Moser. Harris was not pleased with the illustrations here, especially those of the animals. In 1895, a second edition appeared in which A. B. Frost did the illustrations, and the author was ecstatic in his response and appreciation. He wrote:

> But it would be no mystery at all if this new edition were to be more popular than the old one. Do you know why? Because you have taken it under your hand and made it yours. Because you have breathed the breath of life into these amiable brethren of wood and field. . . .
>
> The book was mine, but now you have made it yours, both sap and pith.[24]

The stories in the first book are fragmentary, as well they might be, because they are told at a single sitting; the average story numbers three pages.

Nights with Uncle Remus: Myths and Legends of the Old Plantation appeared in 1883. This book contains 71 stories, the most copious collection to be found in any of the volumes. In length, they are similar to those of the first book. One obvious feature of this collection is its variety in type and differences in dialect as middle Georgia is contrasted with the coastal regions. This seems to be proof—if further proof were needed—that Harris had tapped new sources.

Daddy Jake the Runaway and Short Stories Told After Dark was published in 1889. A third of this book, the first eighty-two pages, narrates the episode of Daddy Jake who ran away from the Gaston Plantation and who because of their love for him was pursued by Lillian and Lucien, children of Mr. Gaston. After Daddy Jake's rescue is related, thirteen stories follow. In the initial pages of the book, "Crazy Sue" tells an animal story. She does not appear in any of the other books.

In chronological order, the next book was *Uncle Remus and His Friends*, 1892. Here Uncle Remus takes a bow and formally announces his intention of retiring from story-telling:

> . . . the old man will bother the public no more with his whimsical stories. Uncle Remus has found out for me many friends in all parts of the world. Thousands of people whom I shall never meet—thousands of little children whom I shall never see, have sent me the most precious tokens of appreciation. It is not an easy nor a pleasing ceremony to step from behind the curtain, pretending to smile and say a brief good-by for Uncle Remus to those who have been so free with their friendly applause. . . . Therefore, let Uncle Remus's good-by be as simple as his stories; a swift gesture that might be mistaken for a salutation as he takes his place among the affable Ghosts that throng the ample corridors of the Temple of Dreams.[25]

Harris here states his primary purpose:

> The stories in this volume were written simply and solely because of my interest in the stories themselves, in the first place, and, in the second place, because of the unadulterated human nature that might be found in them. As I wrote them with my own children around me, or with their voices sounding not far away, I seemed to see other children laughing as the homely stories were read to them; I seemed to see gray-haired children smiling, if they found here, close to earth, a stroke of simplicity ringing true to life; and it

seemed to me that these visions, vain though they might be, were more promising than a hopeless journey through the wilderness to discover at what hour the tribes of the mountains and citizens of the plains shook their hairy fists at each other, and went jabbering their several ways.[26]

In 1903, the public heartily welcomed another Uncle Remus book. Having bade farewell in *Friends,* Harris felt the necessity of explaining Uncle Remus's reappearance; thus the first selection in the new book, *Told by Uncle Remus,* is "The Reason Why." In this exposition he says that the main reason why Uncle Remus retired from the business of story-telling was that the little boy to whom he told the stories had grown to be a very big boy. In the course of time, however, the man who had been the little boy for ever so long came to have a little boy of his own, "and then it happened in the most natural way in the world that the little boy's little boy fell under the spell of Uncle Remus who was still hale and hearty in spite of his age."[27]

The most striking difference noted between this and the four books which had previously appeared is in the length of the stories. Sixteen stories make up the 276 pages, ranging in length from 10 to 25 pages. One also detects a flagging in the interest in the stories which might have been obvious to the author, for he remarks that to the little boy "enthusiasm for the stories came by degrees." As the little boy is slow to warm up to these stories, so is the general reader.

In a letter to James Whitcomb Riley, Harris said:

I haven't been doing much this year besides the new Remus stuff—and I have a suspicion that it isn't quite up to the old mark. I had in my notebook a number of unverified outlines of stories, which I had thrown aside. But some one sent me a copy of Heli Chatelaine's book on Angola, and in that I have verified every outline that I had practically thrown away. The book lay about the house for months and months before I opened it, and then I found what a treasure I had discovered.[28]

It may be that here Uncle Remus strays too far from the story to comment on the boy's health, or to marvel at his mother's system of education. Once when in deep meditation, Uncle Remus is trying to analyze her type. In answer to the little boy's inquiry, Uncle Remus answers, "I wuz des tryin' fer ter count how many diffunt kinder people dey is in dis big worl', an' fo' I got mo' dan half done wid my countin' a pain struck me in mizry an' I had ter break off."

The Tar-Baby and Other Rhymes of Uncle Remus appeared in 1904. The author's note is important:

With the exception of the Tar-Baby story and one other, all the folk-lore stories herein embodied are new, having come into my hands from various sources during the past ten years. The Tar-Baby story has been thrown into a rhymed form for the purpose of presenting and preserving what seems to be the genuine version. Those who care for the narratives themselves will no doubt overlook the somewhat monotonous character of the verse.

In this book are twenty-seven ballads, mostly folk-tales in verse. Plantation and revival songs which had appeared in the first book are also included with one addition, "A Howdy Song". Some of these selections are of a reflective nature; one particularly, "It's Good to Be Old if You Know How to Do," seems to reveal Harris's mystical tendencies. This was written after the death of one of his grandchildren, Charles, the son of Julia Collier Harris and Julian Harris. Harris had become very much attached to the child, whose death affected him greatly.

It is significant that D. Appleton & Company, which had brought out the first book containing the Tar-Baby story in prose, should now publish the volume which contained the story in verse. This was a holiday edition beautifully illustrated by Frost and Kemble. After Appleton had obtained the rights for its publication, Mr. Appleton wrote Harris of his own elation and remarked incidentally that the first Uncle Remus had an annual sale of four thousand copies over a period of twenty years.

A notice in *The New York Times* "Book Review", October 15, 1904, inspired James Whitcomb Riley to send Harris a poem on the new Uncle Remus Book. The notice in *The New York Times* reads: "The publishers of Joel Chandler Harris's new volume of verse, 'The Tar-Baby and Other Rhymes' of Uncle Remus, D. Appleton & Co., state that the advance orders for the book have been so large that three binding orders have been necessary in order to meet the requirements of the trade." [29] James Whitcomb Riley's nephew wrote to members of the Harris family that his uncle used to keep a copy of the *Tar-Baby Rhymes* handy, "and night after night in the last invalid years of his life he read and re-read and re-re-read these verses. I know that at the last of his life it was the favorite of all his books." [30]

Uncle Remus and Brer Rabbit was published by Frederick A. Stokes in 1906. Of the eleven stories, five are in poetry. Though Brer Rabbit says in one of these stories, "being ez populous [popular] es what I is," Harris seems to have lost much of that which was refreshing in the first books. Perhaps the store of plots had become exhausted, or he had not had the time for this work which he enjoyed most.

Uncle Remus and the Little Boy was the title of the book which came out in 1910. There is no formal Introduction to this one, no explanation or reasons for presentation. Evidently, it was intended primarily for juveniles. It must have been an extremely popular edition, because there were ten printings between 1910 and 1919. There are thirteen divisions of the book—all are not stories. There are noticeably fewer philosophical surmisings, and six of the productions are written in rhyme—three of them songs. Two of the incidents revolve around Biblical characters, Joshua and Job. One of the stories, "Hello House," is a poetic version of "Heyo-House" found in *Friends*.

The next Uncle Remus book in the sequence is *Uncle Remus Returns*, 1918. This was published after Harris's death. The stories had formerly appeared in the *Metropolitan Magazine* during 1905-1906. Of the selections in the book there are but six stories, told to the same little boy who appears in *Told by Uncle Remus*. Sketches include "Uncle Remus Falls a Victim to the Mumps", "Views on Church Collections", "Views on Political Theories", and "Uncle Remus Discusses the True Inwardness of Mules".

The latest Uncle Remus book to be published is *Seven Tales of Uncle Remus*, 1948. Although some of these stories have never appeared, they were probably written about 1889. Dr. Thomas H. English, Curator of the Harris Collection at Emory University, who is responsible for the current publication writes:

> As a part of Emory University's contribution to the observance of the centennial (1848-1948) of the birth of Joel Chandler Harris, Litt. D. '02, the *Emory Sources & Reprints* present seven hitherto uncollected tales of Uncle Remus. The first five appeared in special Christmas and Easter issues from 1889 to 1892 of an Atlanta publication entitled *"Dixie": A Monthly Record of Southern Industrial Possibility and Development,* for which they were "written expressly." The last two were found among the manuscripts placed by Mr. Harris's family in the Joel Chandler Harris Memorial Collection of the Emory University Library, a description of which is also included in this number.
>
> Although the contributions to "Dixie" were never printed in a collection of Uncle Remus tales, it appears that it was the author's original intention that they should be. Among the papers in the Memorial Collection are five leaves containing the stories torn from copies of the magazine. The tales are numbered XXV to XXVIII, and bear many proof corrections and emendations in Mr. Harris's hand, though the revision is not thoroughgoing. Eventually four of the tales were taken out of the Negro dialect and retold in *Little Mr.*

Thimblefinger (1894). The fifth, "How Brother Bear Exposed Brother Rabbit at the Barbecue", never reappeared.

Of the two stories that remained in manuscript, one was taken out of the Negro dialect and retold as "Why the Bear is a Wrestler" in *Mr. Rabbit at Home* (1895), the second of the Thimblefinger series. The other has not been found to have been printed in any form.[31]

The preface of *Little Mr. Thimblefinger,* "A Little Note to a Little Book," may furnish grounds for conjecture as to why the tales failed of final inclusion in the Uncle Remus cannon:

> "The stories that follow belong to three categories. Some of them were gathered from the negroes, but were not embodied in the tales of Uncle Remus, because I was not sure they were negro stories . . . . "[32]

The ten Uncle Remus books, though varying in a few aspects, have the same substance—there is the same pattern of the old man as principal raconteur and the little boy as listener; there is the same consistency of the human characters; there is the same atmosphere of reality environing these characters; and there is the same philosophy of the genial Uncle Remus whose treasury of anecdote is rich and distinctive. Harris had the genius to preserve the legends most of which he had imbibed during his youth, but he had also the gift of vivid characterization. Uncle Remus is one of the great products of American literature. The first books had immediate and widespread success and projected their author before readers of every part of America and some foreign countries. From a purely artistic standpoint Harris's books must always be included among the masterpieces of American literature.

IV

TRICKSTER TALES

"Ef I ain't mighty much mistaken, honey, you wanter know how come Brer Rabbit kin outdo de yuther creeturs when he ain't got no tushes ner no claws, an' not much strenk' . . . Well, dat's de ve'y identual thing dat de tales is all about."—Uncle Remus Returns.

NEVER HAS THE TRICKSTER BEEN BETTER EXEMPLIFIED than in the Brer Rabbit of Harris. He presents him as the child of the plantation, but in reality he is many years older. He is as old as the earliest folk tales of the most primitive peoples. Adolf Gerber has traced fifty of the Uncle Remus tales to direct sources in the Old World, some of which bear such close resemblances to the stories in the Uncle Remus series that Gerber remarks, "The resemblances among the stories mentioned . . . are so close that Harris might be accused of having manufactured his on the African patterns, were he not supposed to be a reliable and honest man." [1]

It is not within the scope of the present volume to inquire into the origin of the Uncle Remus tales. However, some idea of the subject may be gathered from Professor

Gerber's very important article, "Uncle Remus Traced to the Old World". In his opinion the majority of the stories were imported from the Old World. He believed that the more complex a story is, the more likely that it has been imported. Basing his study on that theory, he arrives at certain conclusions by examining the tales.

The leading topic of most animal tales which he examined, at least outside of India, is cunning and craft over brute force. In India, the jackal ranks first as a cunning animal and the hare second. In the medieval animal epics and almost everywhere in the folklore of Europe, the fox is the cunning animal. In Africa, the four cunning animals are the jackal, fox, hare, and tortoise. In Brazil, the crafty animal is the cotia, a species of tortoise.

Gerber investigates certain tales that he believes have African origin. There are eight of these stories, six of which are Kaffir tales. He has a group in which the similarities are not so clear, though still beyond doubt variants; sixteen stories comprise this group, two of which are from the Island of Mauritius.

After the general discussion of origins and variants Gerber specifically analyzes the Tar-Baby story. He finds similar stories in Canada, in the West Indies, the Bahama Islands, Brazil, Mauritius, and South Africa.

The next section of Gerber's discussion analyzes stories that can be traced to Europe. These he divided into two groups—those which have their counterparts in modern folklore, and those which may be derived from medieval sources. He traces eight to modern European folk-tales, and seven to the middle ages (these he traces very carefully). Later he mentions five which he cannot trace at length to literary sources. He then enumerates the stories included in the Uncle Remus books for which he found no parallel whatever in the Old World. They are:

N.U.R. 5.—The story of the deluge brought about by the crawfish.

N.U.R. 11.—How Mr. Rooster lost his dinner, and why the chickens are always scratching.

N.U.R. 21.—Animals coasting down a smooth rock induce another, which does not know how, to do the same.

N.U.R. 33.—The guinea-fowl assists the cow against the lion and becomes speckled.

N.U.R. 66.—Two animals try which of them can remain longest without food.

U.R. 7.—An animal in a hollow tree deceives another which is guarding the hole.

N.U.R. 1.—Brer Fox mistakes some white laundry for Miss Goose and tries to run off with it.

14

N.U.R. 51.—One animal burns another in a hole which is supposed to contain honey.

N.U.R. 17.—One animal gets another into trouble by burning off some grass.

N.U.R. 61.—Brer Rabbit runs off with Mr. Dog's shoes.

N.U.R. 64.—Brer Buzzard, who trusts in the Lord, gets self-confident Mr. Hawk for his breakfast.

N.U.R. 70.—Brer Rabbit robs Brer Fox's fish-trap.

Few writers have dealt so comprehensively with a discussion of the Uncle Remus stories as has Gerber, but one finds illuminating comments on some of the stories in an Introduction to a book of Jamaican lore.[2] It is significant that Brer Rabbit, so characteristic a figure of African folklore and the principal character in the legends of Uncle Remus, is found in but two of the stories in this Jamaican collection, and in these one does not recognize anything of his traditionally crafty character. In Jamaica the crafty animal is Annancy, a spider.

Since so many of the stories center around Brer Rabbit,

it is enlightening to note Harris's various descriptions of him and his activities.

BRER RABBIT

"Ef you git any mo' sense, Son Riley Rabbit, you'll be de ruination er de whole settlement."—*Nights with Uncle Remus.*

Descriptions of this crafty "creetur" are scattered throughout the ten books. We first meet him as "dat ar hoppity-skippity, dat ar up-en-down-en-sailin' 'roun' Brer Rabbit." It seems as if he was "born little so he can cut up capers and play pranks no matter wharbouts you put 'm." "In one way anudder he wuz all de time a-pesterin' de yuther creeturs, pullin' der tails an' runnin' off, er makin' jokes 'bout 'im, er playin' pranks on um." Like Mr. Pickwick he was usually producing a constant succession of the blandest and most benevolent smiles, but if these did not delude his victims, he used his feet or his head. "Und' his hat, ef he had enny, Brer Rabbit had a mighty quick thinkin' apple-ratus." "What he can't do wid his foots, he can do wid his head, an' when his head git 'im in trouble dat's deeper dan what he counted on, he puts his 'pen'ence in his foots, kaze dat's whar he keeps his blickity-blick."

He is always engaged in knavish tricks for his own profit or amusement. He is a clever thief—his roguery is generally successful whether it be in getting milk to feed his family or in nibbling up the butter. Unlike Annancy, whose character is consistently bad, Brer Rabbit has some redeeming qualities among which are his cheerfulness and his winning ways. Because of these traits, even the animals who have been duped by him once continually fall prey to his urbanely persuasive manner. "Brer Rabbit he up an' 'low dat dey ain't no dull times wid him, kaze it look like he got sump'n n'er fer ter do every minnit er de day whedder he's at home or whedder he's abroad."

Always he is surrounded by animals stronger physically than himself who should apparently triumph over him; but his suavity ensures the success of his ruses; at the critical moment he displays some art which beguiles them. He even overcomes the king of the forest. When the little boy remarks to Uncle Remus that the Lion couldn't catch Brer Rabbit, Uncle Remus responds, "Now, you talkin', honey—'long side Brer Rabbit ole Brer Lion ain't knee high ter a duck. He mighty strong; he mighty servigrous; but when it come ter head-work he ain't nowhar." Of this headwork Brer Rabbit is understandably vain. "Atter he done make way wid ole Brer Lion, all de yuther creeturs say he sholy is a mighty man, en dey treat 'im good. Dis make him feel so proud dat he bleedz ter show it, en so he strut 'roun' like a boy when he git his first pa'r er boots."

He seems to take on human character, and after one reads a few of the stories, one expects to see him "smokin' his seegyar," "chawin' his terbacker," when highly elated "jumpin' up an' crackin' he heels tergedder," and in the evening, "goin' home to his fambly, same ez enny udder man." Upon one occasion after he has succeeded in taking the house from the other animals—the house which they had built, "he des tuck'n shot [shut] up de house en fasten de winders, en den he go ter bed, he did, en pull de coverled up 'roun' he years [ears], en he sleep like a man w'at ain't owe nobody nuthin'; en needer do he owe um, kaze ef dem yuther creeturs gwine git skeered er run off fum der own house, w'at bizness is dat er Brer Rabbit?"

Nevertheless when he begins to feel so sure of his power something usually happens. "Ebe'y once in a while sump'n er nudder 'ud happen fer ter take de starch out'n Brer Rabbit; hit allers happens dat away. Go whar you will or when you may, en stay ez long ez you choosen to stay, en right dar en den you'll sholy fin' dat folks w'at gits full er cansate [conceit] en proudness is gwine git it tuck out'n um." Several times he gets in tight places and is outdone—by the terrapin or the partridge. In such cases he seems to have more respect for these particular creeturs, and later befriends them or sometimes takes one to be his partner, as he did several times in the case of the terrapin. "De few times what he been outdone he mighty willin' fer ter let um talk 'bout it, ef it'll do um enny good. Dem what outdo 'im got de right ter brag, en he ain't make no deniance un it." When despite his contrivances, he is pursued, "all he ax anybody is ter gin 'im han'roomance, en dem what kin ketch 'im is mo' dan welly-come ter take 'im." At these times, "he picks up de miles wid his feet an' draps um off ag'in des lak dog sheds fleas."

One must not overlook his versatility, nor fail to take cognizance of his talents—"he was no great hand at de fiddle like Mr. Ram, yet he was a drummer, a capital singer, and could perform on the quills." This musical ability he uses to win King Deer's daughter. When Miss Meadows en' de gals think they are going to be disappointed by Mr. Ram, they engage Brer Rabbit as the "patter" for the dance.

He delights in "flinging some sass back" whenever the creeturs molest him. Furthermore, he has his own ideas about most things. When the other animals are planning a contest to see which can laugh the most, Brer Rabbit says he doesn't believe in "company sniggling"; and when he wants to laugh, he has a place where he does his giggling. They are all anxious to know where the place is. In this case, as in most others, they are gullible, and true to his word Brer Rabbit does his giggling but it is at some other creetur's expense. "He des lay down dar en de brier patch en roll en laugh twel his sides hurtid 'm. He bleedzd ter laff. Fox atter 'm, Buzzard atter 'm, en Cow atter 'm, en dey ain't kotch 'im yit."

His tricks are almost as varied as the number of stories in which he appears; therefore no attempt will be made to enumerate all of his cunning episodes. Synopses of a few tales will serve as illustrations:

1. "Brother Fox Catches Mr. Horse" (*Nights,* p. 8). He ties Brer Fox's tail to the tail of a sleeping horse then arouses the horse. Brer Fox receives a kick in the stomach and if the string had not broken would have received more.
2. "Miss Cow Falls a Victim to Mr. Rabbit" (*S. and S.,* p. 41). Miss Cow falls a victim to his craft. She has refused him milk; he asks her to knock down some persimmons for him. In doing so she has to butt the trees, since the persimmons are green, and runs her horns through the tree and cannot pull them out again. When he is satisfied of her helplessness, he gets his family and milk buckets, comes back and milks the cow.
3. "Brother Fox and the White Muscadines" (*Nights,* p. 357). He induces Brer Fox to get in a tree to eat white muscadines and promises to catch him when he jumps, then pretends he has a thorn in his foot and allows Brer Fox to land on the ground so hard that he cannot walk for a long time.
4. "How Mr. Rabbit Saved His Meat" (*S. and S.,* p. 98). He makes away with a cow left in his keeping and covers up his theft by cutting off the tail and planting it in the ground.
5. "Old Grinny-Granny Wolf" (*Nights,* p. 314). He persuades Brer Wolf's grandmother to get in a pot of boiling water to be rejuvenated; when she is dead, he puts on her hide and pretends to be her until the children discover him.
6. "Brother Rabbit Gets Brother Fox's Dinner" (*Nights,* p. 339). He offers to assist Brer Fox, whose dinner has been placed aside, to nail shingles on a roof; he works so effectually that he nails not only the shingles but also Brer Fox's tail.

V

THE OTHER "CREETURS"

"What folks call tricks is creetur sense."
—Uncle Remus and His Friends.

In all the stories there is the same concept of the animal community and familiar colloquies between the animals which mark them as a neighborly group. There are the characteristic acknowledgements as they meet each day, "Howdying" and "spondin'." Of course if one "howdied" and the other refused to "spond'," then there was trouble in the community and they "put der heads togedder an' colloqued an' confabbed." They frequently "passed de time er day wid de nabors" and "always axed 'bout de fambly connexshuns." Of course, "dey dunno de diffunce 'twix what's dern an' what ain't dern . . . dey see what dey want, en dey git it by hook er crook." In this respect they are supposed to be different from folks, "Creeturs kin take what ain't dern, en tell fibs en dey don't no harm come fum it; but when folks tries it, dey er bleedz ter come ter some bad end."

There is romance in the animal kingdom. Often the creeturs "go co'tin en sparklin' 'roun' de naberhood mo' samer dan fokes." After listening to a proposal one of the creeturs "got red in de face, an' den she got white. She think one way an' den she think an'er; she got mad an' den she got glad, an' den she had de all-overs, des lak gals does dez days when some un ax um ter have um."

Not only do they possess much of that cordiality which Harris termed "neighbor knowledge" but they think and act in much the same way as human beings. This attitude makes it easy to forget the outward distinctions when they appear as actors in the stories. They have a type of education:

> "Take um up one side en down de yuther, en all 'roun' ez fur ez dey go, en dey got much sense ez folks. Dey ain't got law sense, en dey ain't got buyin' en sellin' sense, but what dey want wid it? Tell me dat! De ole cow, she wanter git in de sallid patch, en she know how ter open der gate. De ole sow want ripe plums, en she shake de tree; she want corn, en she bump 'er head 'gainst de planks en shatter it out. What mo' do dey want? Dey done got der eddycation." [1]

The animals that are represented in these stories in addition to the rabbit are the fox, the opossum, the bull, the cow, the billy-goat, the wolf, the lion, the frog, the bear, the deer, the alligator, the snake, the wildcat, the mink, the weasel, the pig, the ram, the dog, the terrapin, the polecat, and the turtle. The birds and fowls are the partridge, the hawk, the sparrow, the goose, the chickens, the buzzard, and the guinea-fowls.

Brer Rabbit is King of the Creetur World. In analyzing the Uncle Remus books, it will be useful to determine the tales in which Brer Rabbit is trickster, the few in which he is tricked, and also to record the other animals who appear in the role of tricksters. Brer Rabbit is the mischievous creetur in more than eighty of the stories.[2]

Next in importance as a trickster is the terrapin. There may be many reasons why he plays so conspicuous a part.

There are factors which lend themselves to cunning and craft—his shell, which no animal could penetrate; his ability to live for a long time without food; his silence; the extreme slowness and caution of his movements; his peculiar air of "dogged determination" with which he sets about overcoming or circumventing obstacles. He is the winner in eight of the tales:

1. "Mr. Rabbit Finds His Match at Last." S. *and* S., p. 86.
2. "Mr. Terrapin Shows His Strength." S. *and* S., p. 174.
3. "Mr. Fox Tackles Old Man Tarrypin." S. *and* S., p. 58.
4. "Brother Terrapin Deceives Brother Buzzard." *Nights*, p. 74.
5. "Old Brother Terrapin Gets Some Fish." *Nights*, p. 373.
6. "The Pimmerly Plum." *Nights*, p. 223.
7. "Brother Wolf Still in Trouble." *Nights*, p. 274.
8. "Brother Fox Covets the Quills." *Nights*, p. 79.

Other animals who appear as Tricksters, beside the rabbit and the terrapin, and the stories in which they figure are the following:

I. The Turkey Buzzard
   1. "Mr. Rabbit Meets His Match Again." S. *and* S., p. 103.
   2. "The Story of the Doodang." *Little Boy*, p. 13.
   3. "Mr. Fox is 'Outdone' by Mr. Buzzard." S. *and* S., p. 36.
   4. "Mr. Hawk and Brother Buzzard." *Nights*, p. 362.

II. Bird
   1. "The Wise Bird and the Foolish Bird," *Nights*, p. 370.

2. "A Story About the Little Rabbits." *S. and S.*, p. 107.
3. "Mrs. Partridge Has a Fit." *Friends*, p. 54.
4. "The Most Beautiful Bird in the World." *Returns*, p. 127.

III. Goat
1. "Mr. Benjamin Ram and His Wonderful Fiddle." *Nights*, p. 44.
2. "Mr. Benjamin Ram Defends Himself." *Nights*, p. 291.
3. "Brother Billy Goat Eats His Dinner." *Friends*, p. 112.

IV. Crickett
1. "Little Mr. Cricket and the Other Creatures." *Told By*, p. 87.
2. "The Story of Brer Fox and Little Mr. Cricket." *Little Boy*, p. 152.

V. Bull Frog
"Mr. Bear Catches Old Mr. Bull-Frog." S. *and* S., p. 115.
2. "Mr. Fox and the Deceitful Frogs." S. *and* S., p. 68.

VI. Fox
1. "A Dream and a Story." *Nights*, p. 95.
2. "Brother Fox Makes a Narrow Escape." *Nights*, p. 377.

VII. Bear
1. "How the Bear Nursed the Little Alligator." *Nights*, p. 344.

VIII. Pole-Cat
1. "Brother Bear's Big House." *Brer Rabbit*, p. 11.

IX. Mud-Turtle
   1. "Brother Mud-Turtle's Trickery." *Friends,* p. 167.

X. Snake
   1. "The Cunning Snake." *Nights,* p. 255.

PROPER NAMES OF ANIMALS IN THE TALES

Proper names of other than those of the animal with the prefix Mr. and Brer are not common in the Remus tales. There are, however, a few which are not confined to the principal actors in the stories. Most of the animals are addressed as Mr. or Brer. I divide the proper names into three classes. First, those of creatures of fantasy: Miss Meadows en de gals, Miss Motts, Wull-er-de-Wust, Spewter-Splutter, Mammy-Bammy-Big-Money, Taily-po and Impty-Umpty. Secondly, names formed from appellatives of animals: Rabbit—Miss Bunny Bush-Tail, Miss Molly Cotton-Tail, Riley Rabbit, Miss Molly Har'; Wolf—Wiley-Wolf, Grinny-Granny Wolf, and Mizzle-Mazzle. Thirdly, names given to animals without any apparent reason: Dog—Ramboo, Bamboo, Lamboo, Minny-Minny Morack, Follerlinsko, Birch, Brinjer and Blue; Goat—Mr. Benjamin Ram; Bird—Heeltap, Deeltap; Bear—Klebs, Kibs; Pig—Runt, Grunt; Squirrel—Biggidy-Dicky-Big-Boy; Fox—Tobe; Owl—Billy Big-Eye, Tommy Long-Wing.

This chapter has dealt chiefly with the cunning of the master trickster Brer Rabbit, "mos' inginner'ely all de time, de pranks he played on de yuther creeturs—pestered um bofe ways—a comin' an' a gwine." Harris has kept throughout the same concept of the animal community and the logical coherence of the animal colloquies. No summary of Harris's treatment of the creeturs is better than the one which he wrote in reference to Kipling's *Jungle Book*: "Since the days of Uncle Aesop the animals have been parading about and making speeches, sometimes feebly and sometimes to good purpose; but never have they been caught in the act, as it were, by a more facile or a stronger hand. . . . "[3]

VI

MYTHS

Fer dat what you know mighty certain an' sho',
Ain't mo' dan a thimbleful ter what you ain't know.
—Tar-Baby and Other Rhymes of Uncle Remus.

STITH THOMPSON DEFINES MYTHOLOGY STORIES AS THOSE dealing with the world before it was in the present state. "They explain origin of animals or tribes, or objects or ceremonies or the universe itself."[1] The Myths in the Uncle Remus series follow this definition.

There are twenty-four myths in the ten Uncle Remus books. One concerns man—"Why the Negro is Black." Four treat of natural phenomena—"The Origin of the Ocean", "Where the Harrycane Came From", "Why the Moon's Face Is Smutty", and "Brer Rabbit Has Trouble with the Moon." Five are about birds and fowls—"Why the Turkey Buzzard Is Bald-Headed", "Why the Hawk Catches Chickens," "Why the Guinea-Fowls Are Speckled", "How Mr. Rooster Lost His Dinner" (Why the Rooster Scratches), and "Why the Guineas Stay Awake." Eleven deal with animals—"Why Mr. Possum Has no Hair on His Tail", "How Mr. Rabbit Lost His Fine Bushy

Tail", "When Brother Rabbit Was King", "Brother Rabbit and Brother Bull-Frog", "How Mr. Lion Lost his Wool", "Why Mr. Dog Is Tame", "Why Brother Bull Growls and Grumbles", "Why Brother Fox's Legs Are Black", "Why Brother Bear Has No Tail", "Why Mr. Possum Loves Peace", and "Mr. Goat's Short Tail." Two tell about insects—"Why Mr. Cricket Has Elbows on his Legs", "Jacky-My-Lantern". One has to do with alligators—"Why the Alligator's Back Is Rough".

SUMMARIES OF MYTHS

1. "Why the Negro is Black" (*S. and S.*, p. 163—There was a time when everybody was black. Later, news is circulated around that there is a pond in which one can bathe and become white. The most supple people get in the pond first and come out white; those who are next in suppleness come out mulattoes. These two groups use up nearly all the water. When the remainder of the people come to the pond the most that they can do is " . . . ter paddle about wid der foots en dabble in it wid der han's"—thus these people remain black, the only white parts of their bodies being those which touched the water—the palms of their hands and the soles of their feet.

2. "The Origin of the Ocean" (*Nights*, p. 334)—A rabbit and a lion go hunting; they camp out during the night. While the lion is asleep, the rabbit puts hot embers on him; the lion jumps across the creek and the rabbit cuts the string that holds the banks together. The banks keep falling back, and the creek keeps getting wider and wider; "fum dat day to dis de big waters bin rollin' 'twix' um."

3. "Where the Harrycane Comes From" (*Friends*, p. 39)—Mr. Swamp Owl is appointed by the birds to watch the victuals; he goes to sleep; the victuals are stolen. Thereafter, every time he shows his head in the day-light, they fight him. This makes ole Sis Swamp Owl angry, so she

decides to give the other animals some trouble by starting a hurricane. "She stretch out 'er wings—en flop um down . . . de tree leafs 'gun ter rustle. She flop um some mo' en de lim's 'gun ter shake, en de win' kotch up mo' win' . . . Den de thunder en de lightnin' dey jin'd it, en it des went a-whirlin' . . . en dar's yo' harrycane."

4. "Why the Moon's Face Is Smutty" (*Friends*, p. 130)—In the olden days when the moon wanted to make a change, she would come down and get behind a big poplar log, because she did not want anyone to see her. One day a man is going through the woods carrying charcoal; he does not whistle, as people generally do to warn others that they are approaching, and before he realizes it he comes right upon the moon while she is changing. There is a big "flutterment" as the moon tries to get out of the way; she trips and falls right on top of the bag of charcoal. You can see the signs today—she looks as if she had been hit across the face with a sut bag.

5. "Brer Rabbit Has Trouble with the Moon" (*Little Boy*, p. 34)—Unk' Moon isn't feeling well—wants to send word to Mr. Man that he has caught cold from being out in the night air shining for him and he wants to take a recess. Unk' Moon tells Brer Rabbit to take the following message to Mr. Man, "I'm gittin' weak fer ter be mo' strong; I'm gwine in de shade fer ter git mo' light." Brer Rabbit forgets the message and tells Mr. Man that Unk' Moon says: "I'm gittin' weak; I got no strenk'; I'm gwine whar de shadders stay." Mr. Man cannot understand this message and sends the response, "Seldom seed an' soon forgot; when Unk' Moon dies, his foots gits col'." This makes Unk' Moon angry; he takes a shovel and hits the Rabbit on the mouth and splits his lip; Brer Rabbit jumps at Unk' Moon with tooth and claw and leaves the marks on Unk' Moon's face.

6. "Why the Turkey Buzzard is Bald-Headed" (*Told By*, p. 153)—Miss Turkey Buzzard tries to trick Brer Rabbit

by closing him up in a log. He escapes from the log, gets some hot embers, takes them to Miss Buzzard's door and tells her he has brought her some dinner. When she comes out she gets the hot ashes all over her head and neck, the "way she hopp'd 'roun' wuz so scandalious dat folks calls dat kinder doin's de buzzard dance down ter dis day an' time. Some er de ashes got on de little buzzards an' fum dat time on none er de buzzards tribe had any ha'r er fedders on der head an' not much on der neck."

7. "Why the Hawk Catches Chickens" (*Friends*, p. 3)—The sun promises to find food for the hungry hawk if he can ever catch him in bed. When the rooster aids the hawk and finally wakes him in time to find the sun in bed, the sun is angry, and gives the hawk permission to catch chickens.

8. "Why the Guinea-Fowls Are Speckled" (*Night*, p. 193)—Mr. Lion interrupts Sis Cow and the guineas during a "confab." Sis Cow holds her head down and paws in the dirt. The guineas, one by one, run out and fling up the dirt between Mr. Lion and Sis Cow. This blinds Mr. Lion, and permits Sis Cow to kill him. Out of gratitude she wants to do something for the guineas. Their request is that she do something to make it impossible to see them so far through the woods. She fills a pail of milk, then dips her tail in the milk, and sprinkles the milk all over the guineas. They sit in the sun until they are dry, "en fum dat time out dey got dem little speckles un um."

9. "How Mr. Rooster Lost His Dinner" (*Nights*, p 56) (Why the Rooster Scratches)—The fowls of two adjoining plantations have a frolic; Mr. Peafowl announces dinner. When the guests arrive at the table, they see only a huge pile of cornbread—pones piled on top of pones; on the top is a big ash-cake. Mr. Rooster looks at it, turns up his nose, and struts off. The others remain and "go to work on de pile w'at wuz 'parently corn bread en, lo en beholes, dere wuz meat, greens, potatoes, and turnips."

Mr. Rooster who has not gone far hears the ladies making great admiration; he peeps through a crack and sees what he has missed. Ever thereafter, roosters scratch where they think they might find rations—"mo' dan dat, dey'll scratch wid der rations in plain sight."

10. "Why the Guineas Stay Awake" (*Daddy Jake*, p. 118). One night Brer Fox catches the guineas snoring and runs off with one of them. The others are so frightened "dat dey tu'n right pale on de neck en on de gills." Since then, they never "sleep soun' at night."

11. "Why Mr. Possum Has No Hair on His Tail" (*S. and S.*, p. 129)—Brer Rabbit persuades Brer Possum to climb Brer Bear's persimmon tree. Then, Brer Rabbit tells Brer Bear that Brer Possum is in the tree. In trying to make his escape, Brer Possum reaches the fence, Brer Bear grabs him by the tail, and all the hair comes off in Brer Bear's mouth—"Fum dat day ter dis, Brer Possum ain't had no h'ar on his tail; en needer do his chilluns."

12. "How Mr. Rabbit Lost His Fine Bushy Tail" (*S. and S.*, p. 120)—Brer Rabbit inquires of Mr. Fox his secret of catching a big string of fish. Mr. Fox says that all he has to do is to go down to the creek after sun down and sit there until daylight; then he can draw up a whole armful of fish. Brer Rabbit follows instructions, but it is a very cold night, and the water freezes. He tries to release himself, "he make a pull, en he feel like he comin' in two, en he fetch nudder jerk, en lo en beholes, whar wuz his tail?" So that's why one sees the bobtail rabbits in the woods. "Look like dey er bleedzd ter take atter der pa."

13. "When Brother Rabbit Was King" (*Told By*, p. 101) (Why Dogs Developed the Sense of Smell)—The King takes a holiday; Brer Rabbit serves during the day as king. Mr. Dog comes to the kingdom and makes a complaint that he and his "kinnery" are not treated right; Brer Rabbit has the attendants get turpentine and mix it with red pepper and rub it on Mr. Dog from head to heel and "wen

he holler dey run 'im out'n de place whar de king'n' wuz done." Mr. Dog does not return to his kin; they seek him; "De dogs ax how dey gwineter know 'im when dey fin' him, an' dem at de king's house say dey kin tell 'im by de smell, kaze dey put some turkentine an' red pepper on 'im fer ter kill de fleas and kyo bites . . . sence dat day all de yuther dogs been huntin' fer de dog what went ter de king's house—sence dat day an' hour dey been smellin' fer 'im."

14. "Brother Rabbit and Brother Bull-Frog" (*Told By*, p. 205) (Why the Bull-Frog Has No Tail)—Brer Bull-Frog had once caused Brer Rabbit to fall in a pond. Brer Rabbit swears vengeance. When the time comes for Brer Bull-Frog to leave the pond and go to the bog, Brer Rabbit pretends that he is afraid of Brer Bull-Frog and runs into the hollow of a tree. Brer Bull-Frog pursues; Brer Rabbit runs out of the tree, takes his axe and cuts Brer Bull-Frog's tail off. "Sence dat day, none er de frog fambly has been troubled wid tails."

15. "How Mr. Lion Lost His Wool" (*Brer Rabbit*, p. 50)—Brer Rabbit, Brer Fox and Brer Wolf are spectators at Mr. Man's hog-killing. Brer Rabbit announces that he is going to take a warm bath like Mr. Man gave his hog. The boiling water is prepared. Along comes Mr. Lion; he inquires what they are doing; they respond that they are going to take a bath. Mr. Lion says that is just what he needs. They tell him to back into the water; he does so—the water is scalding. He tries to get out, but slips in "plum ter his shoulder blades." He had a mane from his head to the end of his tail but when he gets out of the hot water, all the wool drops off except the bunch around his neck and the little bit on his tail, "an dat 'a' come off ef de tail hadn't a slipped thoo de hole in de barrel."

16. "Why Mr. Dog Is Tame" (*Told By*, p. 230)—Once the dog was as wild as the wolf. Brer Dog and Brer Wolf are very hungry. They agree that the way to get dinner

is first to make a fire. There is the problem of how to get fire. Brer Wolf tells Brer Dog to borrow a chunk of fire from Mr. Man. Brer Dog goes to Mr. Man's home; is mighty "umble-come-tumble." Mr. Man comes to the door with his gun in his hand and inquires Brer Dog's business. The old woman comes to the door with Mr. Man. She thinks Brer Dog looks so humble he would hurt no one; she invites him in, feeds him. After a while, he smells Brer Wolf, raises his head, looks toward the door. This attracts Mr. Man's attention; he looks out, sees Brer Wolf and shoots at him. It occurs to Mr. Man that Brer Dog can be very helpful to him—he can head the cows off when they make a break through the woods, take care of the sheep, warn him when some other creatures are prowling around, be company for him when hunting, and play with the children. So, Brer Dog is welcome at Mr. Man's home. Later, Brer Dog meets Brer Wolf who inquires why he hasn't returned. Dog points to the collar on his neck, but says he is well-fed and happy. Brer Wolf tries the same plan which Brer Dog had used and comes to Mr. Man's house; Mr. Man shoots at him. "Fum dat time on, it 'uz war 'twix Brer Wolf an' Brer Dog."

17. "Why Brother Bull Growls and Grumbles" (*Friends*, p. 81)—This is the story of the beast-husband transformed by means of the word, "Ballybaloo-bill". A little boy watches Brother Bull transform himself into a man and go courting by night; he tells the woman upon whom Brother Bull is calling of his disguise. She doesn't believe the little boy. One night when her lover calls, the little boy uses the word of transformation, and the person becomes Brother Bull. Thereafter Brother Bull is angry with the little boy because he made that "explosure" and pursues him. One day Brother Bull changes into a man and chases the boy who climbs a tree, and drops hot flapjacks on the man whose arms and head fall off and the little boy is saved. Since Brother Bull is not able to punish the boy

who revealed his disguise, he continues to growl and grumble.

18. "Why Brother Fox's Legs Are Black" (*Friends,* p. 77)—Brer Rabbit and Brer Fox go hunting. They catch game, but have no fire upon which to cook the meat. Brer Rabbit tells Brer Fox to go to Mr. Sun, and when he goes down he can get a big chunk of fire. Brer Fox pursues Mr. Sun, but Mr. Sun goes down in a hole in the ground. Brer Fox is angry because he does not get the fire. He decides that he is going to remain until he gets the fire, and he falls asleep. The next morning Mr. Sun has to rise and when he finds Brer Fox in the way, he scorches his legs until they are black—and they are black to this day.

19. "Why Brother Bear Has No Tail" (*Nights,* p. 113) —Brer Tarrypin, Brer Rabbit, and Mr. Mud-Turkle were having a good time at Mr. Mud-Turkle's mill pond. Mud-Turkle and Tarrypin are sliding from the top of a big, slanting rock; Rabbit's fun is in watching them. Mr. Bear comes along, asks what they were doing to have so good a time. They tell him—sliding down the rock. He inquires why Brer Rabbit isn't joining the others. Brer Rabbit winks his eye at Mud-Turkle and Tarrypin and says he is just resting. They ask Brer Bear to join them. He consents. He gets on the rock and "quile he tail und' him an . . . he break off he tail right smick-smack-smove."

20. "Why Mr. Possum Loves Peace (He's Ticklish) (*S. and S.,* p. 11)—Brer Possum and Brer Coon decide to beat up Mr. Dog, but "de ve'y fus pas he [Mr. Dog] make, Brer Possum fetch a grin fum year ter year, en keel over like he wuz dead." Brer Coon has to beat up Mr. Dog by himself; he accuses Brer Possum of being a coward. Brer Possum replies: "I don't mine fightin', Brer Coon, no mo' dan you duz, but I declar' ter grashus ef I can stan' ticklin' . . . 'and down ter dis day, Brer Possum's bound ter s'render w'en you tech him in de short ribs, en he'll

laugh ef he knows he's gwineter be smashed fer it."

21. "Mr. Goat's Short Tail" (*Daddy Jake*, p. 15). A wolf pursues a goat and a dog until they come to a big creek. The dog swims across. Before he leaves the shore, he touches Mr. Goat with his rabbit foot and turns him into a white rock. When he gets on the other side, he tells Mr. Wolf that he dares him to throw that white rock at him. Mr. Wolf throws the rock. "W'en Mr. Goat struck on 'er side de creek, his tail got broke off."

22. "Why Mr. Cricket Has Elbows on His Legs" (*Told By*, p. 19)—In the olden days old Grandaddy Cricket was bigger than an average goat. During hot weather he would stay out in the sunshine and have a good time—playing the fiddle for the fish to dance and teaching the young birds how to whistle. Once when it becomes so cold that he can not remain out of doors, he works his way into a chimney of a house. There he is so comfortable, at night he takes out his fife and "plays away". The children and the mother at the home are pleased, but the father is annoyed. One night the father tells the cricket if he doesn't hush he will pour scalding water on him. The cricket sings:

> "Hot water wil' turn me brown,
> An' den I'll kick yo' chimney down."

The man pours the water which weakens the clay of the hearth, the chimney comes down on the man; when he comes out from the rubbish even the members of his family do not know him. Grandaddy Cricket kicked so hard, "an' kicked so high, dat he onj'inted bofe his legs an' when he crawled out his elbows wuz where his knees ought to be."

23. "Jacky-My-Lantern" (*S. and S.*, p. 156) (Why the Blacksmith hovers between heaven and earth)—The Bad Man tells the blacksmith that he has come for him. The blacksmith begs the Bad Man to make a trade with him:

"At de een 'er one year de sperit er de blacksmif wuz to be his'n en endurin' er dat time de blacksmif mus' put in his hottes' licks in de intruss er de Bad Man, en den he put a spell on de cheer de blacksmif wuz settin' in, en on his sludge-hammer." The next year the blacksmith has his fun and forgets about the trade. Satan returns at the end of the year and having forgotten about the "conjur chair" sits in it. He tells the man if he will release him he will give him another year. The second year when the Bad Man returns, he unwittingly picks up the sledge-hammer; for release he promises the blacksmith another year of freedom. The third year the Bad Man takes the blacksmith, puts him in a bag and starts home. On his way, he stops at a barbecue, puts the sack under the table. While he is gone the blacksmith gets out of the bag and substitutes another bag. The Bad Man gets home and calls all the little devils to come and see what he has brought them. He opens the sack and a big bull dog jumps out. When the blacksmith dies he goes to heaven, but is not acceptable there. He goes to hell; the Bad Man opens the door, recognizes him and says, "You'll hatter skuze me, Brer Blacksmif, kase I dun had speunce 'longer you, you'll hatter go some'rs else ef you wanter raise enny racket." Since that day "de blacksmif bin sorter huv' rin' 'roun' 'twix' de heavens en de ye'th, en dark nights he shine out so fokes call 'im Jacky-my-lantun." [2]

24. "Why the Alligator's Back Is Rough" (*Nights*, p. 141)—Brer Rabbit tells Brer Alligator that he has been in trouble—dogs have been after him. Brer Alligator laughs and says he doesn't know what trouble is; he goes to sleep on the grass. Brer Rabbit decides he is going to show Brer Alligator what trouble is; so he sets the broom-grass afire where Brer Alligator is lying. At first Brer Alligator thinks it is a dream in which he feels the sun shining hot; he wakes up and finds fire all about him and cries, "Trouble! Trouble!" He dashes through the grass, goes to the creek

to quench the burning skin—his back and his tail become shrivelled and have remained so ever since.

Morals are implied in many of the tales but clearly stated in a few, of which two examples follow. A third tale is added as a case of rather obvious implication.

1. "The Story of the Deluge and How It Come About" (*S. and S.*, p. 20)—The animals call a meeting; Mr. Lion presides. There are many controversies during the course of the assembly: in the midst of the wrangling, an elephant tramps on a crawfish. The other crawfish get angry and draw up "a kinder peramble," but nobody hears it, or everybody ignores it, "'ceppin may be de Mud-Turkle en de Spring Lizzud, en der enfloons wuz pow'ful lackin'." Another crawfish is squashed. The other crawfish protest and draw up "anudder peramble wid sum mo' wharfo'es" but still get no audience, so they wink at the Spring Luzzud and the Mud-Turkle and "den dey bo'd little holes in de groun', en went down outer sight." The crawfish bore into the ground until they unloose the fountains of earth. There is a deluge and all the creatures are drowned, "en all bekaze dey let on 'mong deyselves dat dey wuz bigger dan de Crawfishes."

2. "The Fate of Mr. Jack Sparrow" (*S. and S.*, p. 92)—One day Brer Rabbit is sitting under a tree "thinking aloud"—he has come to a decision as to the method he is going to use to show Miss Meadows an' de gals that he is the boss of Brer Fox. Jack Sparrow is up in the tree and hears Rabbit's plan; he declares that he is going to tell Brer Fox. Brer Rabbit knows that he must think of a scheme quickly. He decides that the first one that sees Brer Fox will triumph, so he rushes to Brer Fox and asks, "W'at dis twix' you en me, Brer Fox? I hear tell you gwine ter sen' me ter 'struckshun, en nab my fambly, en 'stroy my shanty." Brer Fox knows he has made no such statement; he gets angry and asks Brer Rabbit who told him that; Brer Rabbit says Jack Sparrow told him. A

little later Jack Sparrow comes along and tries to tell Brer Fox what Brer Rabbit has planned to do to him. Fox eats Jack Sparrow. "Der ain't no way fer ter make tattlers an' tail-b'arers turn out good."

3. "How Old Craney-Crow Lost His Head" (*Told By*, p. 126)—A hurricane lifts Craney-Crow from his roost in a lagoon and takes him to a swamp. He looks around at the birds there and he doesn't see any with heads. (The birds were sleeping with their heads under their wings, but he doesn't know this.) He thinks it is the fashion to sleep without your head and he doesn't want to be out of fashion. He asks Pop-Eye (Brer Rabbit) why the birds sleep without their heads. Rabbit replies that the mosquitoes are so bad in the swamp that the birds who live there are in a habit of taking their heads off at night and putting them in a safe place. Craney-Crow wants to follow the fashion. Rabbit introduces him to Dr. Wolf who, he says, will "commerdate" him. Wolf tells Craney-Crow to hold his head low so that he can perform the operation; when the crow lowers his head, Wolf snaps down on it, "an' dat wuz de las' of dat Craney-Crow. . . . An' dat's de reason dat Craney-Crows all fly so fas' when dey come thoo dis part er de country."

VII

THE SUPERNATURAL: WITCH, GHOST, AND DEVIL TALES

"*Witch, 'e no dead ghos'—'e life folks, wey you shekky han' wit'.*"—Nights with Uncle Remus.

THE SUPERNATURAL ELEMENT OCCURS IN FIFTEEN UNCLE Remus stories. Among the Coastal and Sea Island Negroes there were apparently more survivals of the miraculous than among the group in Middle Georgia. Thus Daddy Jack figures prominently in the supernatural tales, either as narrator or auditor. He has the reputation of being a conjurer, and is frequently sought for his knowledge of charms and counter-charms.

A motif recognizable in several of the stories is that of the "slip-skin" belief; that is, witches slip off their skins during the night to perform their atrocious deeds. This is the dominant theme in "A Plantation Witch" (*S. and S.*, p. 150). Uncle Remus explains, "Hit seem like dat witch fokes is got a slit in de back er de neck, en w'en dey wanter change der se'f dey des pull de hide over de head same ez ef 'twuz a sheet, en dar dey is." In this story a man tells how he cures his brother of being a witch. About midnight each night the witch brother leaves the house in the shape of a bat and goes out to engage in his tricks. One night his brother watches him slip off his skin to assume invisibility. After the witch leaves, the brother turns his skin wrong-side out and sprinkles it with salt. The witch returns several times—first, in the form of a black cat, then as a black dog, and finally as a big black wolf. He grabs the skin and rushes out. A little later his brother hears the witch howling and squalling because the salt is stinging him. Thereafter, he gives up conjuring.

Daddy Jack has his theory about witches. When Aunt Tempy asks him how you can tell whether you are a witch or not, he replies:

> Oo! 'e easy nuff. Wun da' moon is shiun low, wet-a you' han' wit' da' pot-licker grease; rub noung heifer 'pon 'e nose; git 'pon 'e bahck. Mus' hol' um by 'e year; mus' go gallop, gallop down da' lane, tel' e do come 'cross one-a big gully. Mus' holler, "*Double, double, double up! double, double, double up!*" Heifer jump, oona witch; heifer no jump, oona no witch.[1]

"Taily-po" (*Returns,* p. 52) has for motif return for a mutilated, missing portion of the body—here, it is the tail. Brer Rabbit is indignant because Mr. Man is always having his dogs chase him. He visits Mammy-Bammy-Big-Money, the rabbit witch, and asks her assistance. She takes from the wall the hide of some kind of varmint, places it on the floor, sprinkles salt on it; whereupon the hide moves, stretches itself, and takes the form of a big wildcat. Mammy-Bammy-Big-Money then tells Brer Rabbit to go home and assures him that he will have no more trouble. That night Mr. Man is disturbed by a noise. Upon investigation, he observes that a door is open which he is sure he has closed; he closes it again. The wildcat has entered the house and opened the door to an inner room. He is seeking his escape when Mr. Man slams the door and cuts off the wildcat's tail. Mr. Man picks up the tail and flings it in the fire. Later Mr. Man is awakened by a scratching and a gnawing, and a voice sings:

"Taily-po, you know an' I know
Dat I wants my Taily-po!
Over an' under an' thoo de do!
I'm a-comin' fer ter git my Taily-po!

The wildcat gets in the house, finds his tail among the burning embers, sets the house on fire, and rushes out.[2]

Another motif, that of transformation or shape-shifting, is seen in the story of "The Man and the Wild Cattle" (*Friends,* p. 91). One of the wild cattle transforms herself into a woman and marries a hunter. She ties his dogs, Minny-Minny Morack and Follamalinska. The hunter goes to the woods; the wild cattle pursue him; he calls his dogs who fail to respond. He sticks an arrow in the ground from which a tree springs; the hunter climbs to the top of the tree. The wild cattle gets axes and cut the tree down; just as it is about to fall, he sticks another arrow in the ground; a larger tree springs up. Before the wild cattle can cut this one down, the dogs have gnawed the ropes and released themselves; they come to the hunter's rescue. Most of the wild cattle are killed, including a snow-white cow. When the hunter returns home, his wife is not to be found anywhere.

Another story of the type, illustrating the shape-shifting witch-husband, is "Why the Bull Growls and Grumbles" —a story which has already been discussed under the chapter dealing with myths.

"How a Witch Was Caught" (*Daddy Jake,* p. 83) is also a story of transformation in which there is eventual disenchantment. A miller owns a haunted house in which people are afraid to remain all night. However, one night an itinerant preacher who is greatly in need of a room decides that he will spend the night there.

"De preacher man say he des soon stay dar ez anywhar's,

kaze he bin livin' in deze low-groun's er sorrer too long fer ter be sot back by any one-hoss ha'nts."

The miller said: "Ef de preacher man wuz ready fer ter face de ha'nts and set up dar en out blink um, dey wouldn't be nobody in de roun' worl' no gladder dan 'im."

During the night a large black cat appears; the preacher catches it and cuts off one of the toes and wraps it up. The next morning he unwraps the bundle—instead of the toe, there is a finger with a ring on it.

The next morning the preacher goes to bid farewell to the miller and his wife. When he goes to shake hands with the miller's wife she complains of a painful finger on the right hand and extends the left. Her husband says he has never heard her complain of a painful hand before and demands that she extend it. When she does so, the preacher says he believes he can cure it—she puts out her hand, he places the finger with the ring on it, and it fits "smick-smack-smoove." With that, the preacher tells the miller his wife is a witch. The woman yells and covers her head. The preacher says that the only way to cure a witch is to burn her. When they tie her, she turns to a big black cat "en dat's de way she wuz burnt."

"The Little Boy and His Dogs" (*Daddy Jake*, p. 93) is of the same type. Two fine ladies appear at the home of a little boy whose sister has been lost for some time and ask permission for the boy to show them where the big road forks. He is suspicious about the women; however, he consents to go after he has instructed his mother to turn loose his dogs, Minnyminny Morack and Follerlinsko, when the water in the pan turns to blood. The mother follows instructions. On the road the little boy is frightened and climbs a tree. The ladies, who are panthers, convert their tails into axes and are about to cut the tree down when the dogs come to the boy's rescue. They also help him to rescue his sister.

One of the most popular stories featuring an animal

that changes its form is "Uncle Remus's Wonder Story" (*Daddy Jake*, p. 139) frequently known as "The Witch-Wolf". The witch-wolf, Mizzle-Mazzle, likes to eat folk but before she can eat them, she transforms herself into a woman and marries them. On one occasion, her suitor goes to Judge Rabbit for advice as to whether he should marry her. Judge Rabbit advises that he ask the girl several questions, the last of the series should be if she can milk the red cow. The suitor follows instructions. When the girl goes to milk the red cow, the cow bucks, and Mizzle-Mazzle has to jump over the fence. Then the man sees her wolf hoofs.

"The Adventures of Simon and Susanna" (*Daddy Jake*, p. 171) tells how Susanna outwits her witch-father. "The Baby and the Punkins" (*Seven Tales*, p. 18) recounts the transformation of a witch baby into a man.

There are three stories which deal with conjury: "Brother Rabbit's Love-Charm" (*Nights*, p. 198), "Brer Rabbit Causes Brer Fox to Lose His Hide" (*Little Boy*, p. 50), and "The Hard-Headed Woman" (*Told By*, p. 276). In the first, "Brother Rabbit's Love-Charm", Daddy Jack gives Brer Rabbit the recipe for winning the girl whom he loves. The charm bag which he is to wear around his neck is to contain "tusk from an elephant, tooth from an alligator, and a rice bud." Brer Rabbit has to use some of his ruses to secure the ingredients for the bag, but he succeeds. "Brer Rabbit Causes Brer Fox to Lose His Hide" is discussed under "Trickster Stories", but is mentioned here because Brer Rabbit tells Mr. Lion that the reason he has delayed so long in coming to see him during his illness is that he has had to make a journey to Mammy-Bammy-Big-Money to ask a cure for Mr. Lion. The suggested cure is "the hide of his best friend." Mr. Lion roars out: "Fetch me de hide er Brer Fox." "The Hard-Headed Woman" tells of a woman who delights in doing the opposite of whatever her husband requests. The man "spit in de ashes, he did, an' he make a cross-mark, an' turn 'roun' twice so he kin face de sunrise. Den he shuck a gourd vine flower over de pot, an' sump'n tol' 'im fer ter take his res' an' wait twel de moon come up." The pot seems to take feet and chases the woman away.

GHOST STORIES

"Ef anybody got any hard feelin's 'gin' me, I want um ter take it out w'ile deyer in de flesh; w'en dey come a-hantin' me, I'm done—I'm des *done*."

—*Nights with Uncle Remus.*

There are only two ghost stories in the entire series: "A Ghost Story" (*Nights*, p. 161) and "Spirits, Seen and Unseen" (*Nights*, p. 154). Aunt Tempy tells the first:—A woman dies and her friends put two silver dollars (apparently all the money she possesses) on her eyelids to hold them down. Her husband attends her to the grave, takes the two dollars and carries them home with him. That night the woman appears to him, demanding her money—here we have the motif of the ghost who returns for a missing object. "Spirits, Seen and Unseen" is not strictly a story; rather it relates a series of folk beliefs and mentions rumors with regard to spirits. Daddy Jack says that he has seen many ghosts and he isn't afraid of them, "I is a bin-a shoo dem 'pon dey own sied de road; I is a bin-a punch dem 'way wit' me cane."

The following list gives some popular beliefs interspersed in the tales, including ghost-lore, omens and signs, and folk-medicine.

Ghosts

1. W'ence you year chilluns talkin' en gwine on periently wid deyse'f, der er bleedz ter see ha'nts. *Nights*, p. 155.
2. Wun dey [ghosts] call, hol' you' mout' shet. *Nights*, p. 155.

3. 'E berry bahd fer mek answer, wun da' harnt holler. Dem call-a you 'way fum dis lan'. *Nights*, p. 155.
4. W'en you meets up wid one er deze ha'nts, ef you'll tak'n' tu'n yo' coat wrong-sud-outerds, dey won't use no time in makin' der disappearance. *Nights*, p. 156.

Luck

1. Luck in de house whar de cobwebs hangs low. *Nights*, p. 147.
2. Rabbit foot'll gin you good luck. *Nights*, p. 167.

Superstitions

1. When ole Brer Mud-turkle shet down on yo' han', you got ter cut off his head an' den wait twel it thunder 'fo' he turn loose. *Friends*, p. 170.
2. Promise is a promise, dough you make it in de dark er de moon. *Nights*, p. 231.
3. Put yo' han' in a pa'tridge nes', en he'll quit dem premises dough he done got 'lev'm dozen aigs in dar. *Nights*, p. 231.
4. You kin put de shovel in de fier en make de squinch owl hush he fuss. *Nights*, p. 28.
5. You kin go out en put yo' han' on de trees en make deze yere locus'-bugs quit der racket. *Nights*, p. 27.

6. [One of Miss Meadows' gals says that she must have some sign regarding her future husband; she has tried the "spells" mentioned in the paragraph below, but to no avail.]

> . . . I tuck 'n fling a ball er yarn outen de window at midnight, en dey ain't nobody come en wind it. I tuck a lookin'-glass en look down in de well en I ain't see nothin' 't all. I tuck a hard-b'iled egg en scoop de yaller out, en fill it up wid salt en eat it widout drinkin' any water. Den I went ter bed, but I ain't dream 'bout a blessed soul. I went out

'twix' sunset and dark en fling hempseed over my lef' shoulder, but I ain't see no beau yit. *Daddy Jake,* pp. 193-194.

Folk-Medicine

1. Strip er red flannil tied 'roun' yo' arm'll keep off de rheumatiz. *Nights,* p. 167.
2. Stump-water 'll kyo [cure] 'spepsy. *Nights,* p. 167.

DEVIL TALES

"Go git 'm a chunk er fier an' let 'm start a sinner fact'ry er his own."—*Uncle Remus Returns.*

"Impty-Umpty and the Blacksmith" (*Returns,* p. 26) is the only devil tale in the series with the exception of "Jacky-my-Lantern" which has been discussed in the chapter on myths. The story tells of a blacksmith who has a shop at the cross-roads. Brer Rabbit has a habit of going to the shop at night when the blacksmith has gone and sitting by the fire. He usually leaves before the blacksmith comes in the mornings; but one morning he oversleeps, the blacksmith finds him in his shop and throws a hammer at him. This vexes Brer Rabbit, and he thinks of a method of revenge. He tells his friend, Mr. Rickerson-Dickerson, to tell all the creeturs as they pass the shop to say to the blacksmith that he is going to have company.

The blacksmith makes an iron box and says he will be ready for the company when it comes. One night the creeturs are in the shop, and the conversation drifts to Impty-Umpty, "an' ef de ol' Boy had 'a' had any character dey'd 'a' ruint it right den an' dar." The blacksmith says if old Impty-Umpty is going to be the company they are talking of, it is all right with him. At this time a tall black man steps inside the door—his eyes shine like a piece of glass in the moonlight, he has on a stove-pipe hat, a broadcloth suit; he is slim, slick and supple, is club footed and double-jointed. The group is astonished at his appearance especially after he takes up a plow tongue and converts it into a shovel plow. They ask who he is. He replies, "Folks got a heap er diffunt names fer me but I ain't no ways proud, an' so I 'spon's ter all un um. . . . some calls me de Ol' Boy, an' den, ag'in, dey calls me Satan, an' I got wuss soundin' names dan dat."

The blacksmith tells Impty-Umpty that he has heard there are three things which he cannot do—change into a hog, a monkey, or a cat. Impty-Umpty smiles and changes himself successively into a hog, a monkey and a cat. At the last transformation, the blacksmith grabs the cat and fastens him in his iron box and locks it. After a while Brer Rabbit tells the blacksmith that he doesn't believe the cat is yet in the box, urges the blacksmith to open it. He does so and a big black bat flies out and hits the blacksmith in the face. He tries to catch it but he can't. Time goes on and the blacksmith dies:

—I dunno ef it's so er no; it mought be des de hearsay—but dey tells me dat de blacksmiff had 'casion ter go down dar whar Impty-Umpty live at; he mought des been passin' by; leas' ways he went ter Impty-Umpty's house an' knock at de do'. He knock once an' he knock twice, an' den ol' Impty-Umpty holler an' ax 'Who dat?' Blacksmiff say, sezee, "Tain't nobody but me.' Impty-Umpty 'low, he did, 'Ef youer dat blacksmiff what shet de cat up in a box, you can't come in dis place' an' den he call one er his little Impties, an' say, 'Go git 'im a chunk ef fier an let 'im start a sinner fac'try er his own.[3] He can't come in here.' . . . Dat . . . wuz all de fur de tale could foller de blacksmiff.[4]

VIII

PROVERBS AND FOLK-SAY

"Brer Rabbit, he study an' study an' de mo' he study, de wuss he like it."—Told by Uncle Remus.

LORD RUSSELL HAS DEFINED *proverb* AS "THE WISDOM OF many and the wit of one." Archer Taylor asserts, "The definition of a proverb is too difficult to repay the undertaking; and should we fortunately combine in a single definition all the essential elements and give each the proper emphasis, we should not even then have a touchstone." [1] If for our purpose we give the definition in *The New English Dictionary*—"A short, pithy saying in common and recognized use," we should have a definition wide enough to include most of the sayings though the word *short* must be interpreted liberally.

Perhaps the strongest evidence of the inborn wit of the Negro is his ability to express ideas with force and originality. There is no doubt that a people who could make the animal creatures say and do such smart things, first had the smartness and sense themselves. Among the illiterate groups of Negroes there exists today, as in the day of Uncle Remus, an almost uncanny ability to express in a brief striking manner some idea whose rich imagery a well educated person might have pondered for hours with results less telling. Sometimes a whole philosophy is expressed in four or five words; for instance, "If youse black, git back!" [2]

One of the most neglected fields of collection in the realm of Negro folklore is that of proverbs. At present there is no such collection, unless one mentions *Uncle Gabe Tucker,*[3] which does not deal solely with folk-proverbs. With regard to this phase of folklore another observation seems significant; namely, that next to the Annancy stories, the greatest bulk of collected Jamaican lore is the proverbs.[4] It is difficult to account for the large number of collections of proverbs in that island and the almost complete absence of proverbs of the American Negro. It may be that, while the American Negro found outlet for his feelings in the spirituals, the Jamaican Negro found release for his emotions in the proverb. Whatever the case, the fact remains that the proverbs of the American Negro are yet to be mined. Harris himself, who understood so well the Negro's philosophy and was so able to present other phases of his lore with such extraordinary success, devotes only four pages in the eight Remus books to a list of proverbs. I have undertaken to cull from the pages of the stories themselves additional proverbs and proverbial expressions.

There are many expressions found in the books which were probably familiar and entered into the speech of the people; however, in the lists which follow I have endeavored to include only those that are most interesting or picturesque. The classification follows the general divisions of proverbs as given by Professor Harold W. Thompson [5]—proverbs of wisdom and proverbs of poetry (rhetoric).

Of the proverbs of wisdom by far the greatest number is that of ironical and cynical observation:

'Oman [woman] tongue ain't got no Sunday. *Friends*, p. 45.

What fattens de chickens fattens de hawks. *Friends*, p. 3.

You can't make gourd out'n punkin. *Friends*, p. 45.

Drowned fer de want er bofe sense en breff. *Friends*, p. 141.

Blin' hoss better dan no hoss. *Friends*, p. 245.

When de spoon want anything, it hatter go ter de bowl. *Friends*, p. 45.

De bes' kinder bread gits sour. *Nights*, p. 242.

Her clickin' tongue wuz long an' loud an' mighty well hung. *Tar-Baby*, p. 59.

De trufe ain't never been hurted yit by dem what ain't believe it. *Told By*, p. 294.

Sense don't stan' fer goodness. *Friends*, p. 160.

Better be dead dan outer fashion. *Told By*, p. 152.

It takes two ter make a bargain, an' one mo' ter see dat its done all right. *Returns*, p. 122.

Fool fer luck, en po' man fer chillun. *Friends*, p. 154.

Too menny frens spiles de dinner. S. *and* S., p. 59.

Eave-drappers don't hear no good er deyse'f. S. *and* S., p. 54.

I done tuck notice in my time dat what white folks calls sense don't turn out to be sense eve'y day en Sunday too. *Friends*, p. 142.

Dar's a heap er ups an' downs in dis worl', mo' speshually downs. *Little Boy*, p. 34.

Ef eve'ybody wuz ter git all der wishes, de wide worl' 'ud be turned upside down an' rollin' over de wrong way. *Little Boy*, p. 13.

Proverbs of warning:

Dead dog never dies, en cheatin' never th'ives. *Friends*, p. 161.

Nimble heel make restless min'. *Nights*, p. 228.

You hatter harness two horses one at a time. *Returns,* 'Twon't do fer ter give out too much cloff fer ter cut one pa'r pants. *S. and S.,* p. 39.

De place wharbouts you spill de grease,
Right dar youer boun' ter slide,
An' whar you fine a bunch er h'ar,
You'll sholy find de hide. *S. and S.* p. 21.

Dey mo' ways ter fin' out who fell in de mill pond without fallin' in yo'se'f. *Friends,* p. 144.

Proverbs for special occasions:

Don't kick 'fo' you er spurred. *Nights,* p. 122.

Nuff's a nuff, en too much is a plenty. *Nights,* p. 184.

Dey might be more dan one proberbul. *Friends,* p. 263.

Bless us en bine us, en put us in crack whar de Ole Boy can't fine us. *Nights,* p. 153.

Proverbs of comfort and courage:

Any kinder sound egg will hatch ef you gi' it time. *Told By,* p. 161.

A light heart made a long life. *Told By,* p. 178.

Proverbs of poetry or rhetoric "are enjoyed chiefly as imaginative comparison or other description that rises above the commonplace rather to delight than to instruct. The source of delight is not always in sound—alliteration and assonance—nor in picture, polished form, or fanciful thought; because we are Americans, the pleasure sometimes arises from turns of humor." [6]

Indefinitely numerous are the proverbial comparisons based upon adjective, adverbs, noun, or verb found in the Remus books. A partial list follows:

My 'membunce [remembrance] wabblin' 'roun' like a hoss wid de blin' staggers. *Friends,* p. 115.

Des ez frien'ly ez clabber an' whey. *Little Boy,* p. 23.

Sharp ez a bamboo brier. *Friends,* p. 83.

I'm des about ez fat ez de mule de man had, which he hatter tie a knot in his tail fer ter keep 'im fum

slippin' thoo de collar. *Friends,* p. 139.
High ez a poplar tree, en big aroun' ez a gin-house. *Friends,* p. 55.
Des ez smilin' ez a basket er chips. *Friends,* p. 51.
Des ez limber ez a wet rag. *Nights,* p. 66.
Des ez big ez life un twice ez natchul. *Nights,* p. 247.
Des ez gaily ez a race hoss. *Returns,* p. 23.
Des ez ca'm ez a dead pig in de sunshine. *Friends,* p. 247.
Des ez lively ez a cricket in de ashes. *Nights,* p. 99.
Des ez snug ez de ole black cat und' de barn. *Nights,* p. 226.
Des ez frisky ez kittens. *Friends,* p. 47.
Des ez sassy ez a jay-bird. S. *and* S., p. 24.
Des ez soshubble ez a basket er kittens, S. *and* S., p. 26.
Des ez pert ez a circus pony. S. *and* S., p. 37.
Des ez gaily ez a June cricket. S. *and* S., p. 82.
Des ez sassy ez a jay-bird at a sparrer nest. S. *and* S., p. 47.
Come steppin' up same ez ef he wer treddin' on kurkerburrs. S. *and* S., p. 45.
Des ez ezy ez gwine ter sleep in a swing. *Friends,* p. 29.
Dey wuz settin' dar des ez ca'm, en ez cole-blooded ez mud-cats in de mont' er Jinerway. *Friends,* p. 262.
Snorin' same ez somebody filin' a cowhorn. *Friends,* p. 9.
No bigger dan a young rabbit atter de hide been tuck off. *Friends,* p. 47.
Had no mo' heft dan a pa'tridge egg wid de innerds blow'd out. *Friends,* p. 45.
Whole passel er pills what ain't bigger dan a gnat's heart. *Told By,* p. 282.
Lopin' 'long mo' samer dan a bay colt in de bolly-patch. *Nights,* p. 86.
Draw'd hisself up twel he look like he ain't bigger'n a poun' er soap atter a hard day's washin'. *Friends,* p. 138.
Had mo' fun dan a mule kin pull in a waggin. *Told By,* p. 45.

Dey was a heap mo' und' his hat dan what you could git out wid a fine tooth comb. *Told By*, p. 64.

No mo' fuss dan a fedder-bed makes when you let it 'lone. *Told By*, p. 252.

Sno'in away like somebody sawin' gourds. *Friends*, p. 17.

Run 'roun' like a pig wid hot dish-water on his back. *Friends*, p. 27.

Look like de flo'll burn blisters in his feet. *Friends*, p. 95.

Lookin' like de really-truly goodness wuz des drippin' fum his mouf, an' oozin' fum his hide. *Returns*, p. 98.

'Gun ter sno' like he done swaller'd a hoss, mane and huff. *Returns*, p. 101.

His talk soun' like a bummil-eye bee been ketch in a sugar barrel an' can't git out. *Told By*, p. 218.

Runnin' on like a cat-bird in a peach orchard. *Friends*, p. 239.

A-comin' like a pot a-boilin'. *Returns*, p. 24.

[Alligator] His two eyes look des perzackly like two bullets floatin' on de water. *Told By*, p. 252.

Ol' Brer Yalligater float on de water like he ain't weigh no mo' dan one er deze yer postich stamps. *Told By*, p. 254.

Float backerds an' forreds like a tied canoe. *Told By*, p. 255.

Eve'y time he drawed a breff it soun' like somebody wuz trying fer ter grin' coffee. *Returns*, p. 69.

He wuz like a slip thrip—little but ole. *Friends*, p. 179.

Humorous and vigorous metaphor:

W'at does you season your recollection wid fer ter make it hole on so? *S. and S.*, p. 204.

An' how does yo' copperositee seem ter segashuate? [How do you feel?] *Tar-Baby*, p. 9.

Ef dat don't bang my time, Joe's dead an' Sal's a widder. *Friends*, p. 5.

You yeard my horn. *Friends*, p. 247.

You kin des use my head fer a hole in de wall. *Nights,* p. 291.
I'm a punkin ahead er yo' 'simmon. *Friends,* p. 147.
Sence de day my whiskers 'gun to bleach. *Nights,* p. 124.
I'll have dis bread done in two shakes uv a sheep's tail. *Friends,* p. 148.
[He] 'gin 'im leg bail. *Nights,* p. 97.
He swaller de grin en fetch a howl. *Nights,* p. 117.
I got a whole bag full er reasons. *Little Boy,* p. 88.
When it comes to soopleness, I takes it wid me wharsomever I goes. *Little Boy,* p. 36.
Dem what seen one harrycane ain't gwine hone atter no mo'. *Friends,* p. 40.
He kin des snatch dem ole-time chunes fum who lay de rail. *Nights,* p. 45.
Right dar's whar he broke his merlasses jug. *S. and S.,* p. 25.
Right dar's whar he drap his munnypuss. *S. and S.,* p. 27.
S'arch de country fum hen-roost to river-bank. *Nights,* p. 273.
I year tell er one [story] dat'll des natally make de kinks on yo' head onquile deyse'f. *Nights,* p. 161.
She wuz so mad dat she could 'a' bit a railroad track in two. *Told By,* p. 292.
He wuz all de time betwixt a grin an' a giggle. *Told By,* p. 223.
He ain't seed hide ner ha'r er 'im. *Told By,* p. 227.
A pain struck me in my mizry. *Told By,* p. 189.
Somehow er 'nother, by toof er toe-nail. *Returns,* p. 75.
Ef I'd 'a' stayed on dat train, dey wouldn't 'a' been 'nough er me left fer de congregation ter sing a song over. *Told By,* p. 13.
I boun' you stretched yo' guesser. *Told By,* p. 105.
I got ter ramblin' back twel my 'membrunce hit me a

whack dat come mighty nigh knockin' me flat. *Returns,* p. 28.

De ailment what I had, honey, wuz some'rs on de right han' side er my min'. *Returns,* p. 28.

Dat suit him ter a gnat's heel. *Told By,* p. 67.

When it comes ter low-down meanness, she wuz rank an' ripe. *Told By,* p. 288.

He tuck his foot in his han'. *Friends,* p. 88.

When he git ter talkin' he'll stretch his blanket spite er de worl'. *Friends.* p. 123.

Fus an' fo'mus youer thumpin de wrong watermillion. S. *and* S., p. 234.

Youer w'isslin' up de wrong chube. S. *and* S., p. 234.

Extended Metaphors:

Definitions of a phonograph:

1. Hit's one er deze yer kinder w'atzinames w'at sasses back w'en you hollers at it. S. *and* S., p. 230.

2. All yo' gotter do is ter holler at de box, an' dar's yo' remarks. Dey goes in, an' dar dey er tooken an' dar dey hangs on twel you shakes de box an' den dey drops out des ez fresh ez dese yer fishes w'at you gits frum Savannah. S. *and* S., p. 230.

3. Hit's mighty funny unter me how dese folks kin go an' prognosticate der eckoes inter one er deze yer i'on boxes, an' dar hit'll stay on twel de man comes 'long an' tu'ns de handle an' let's de fuss come pilin' out. S. *and* S., p. 230. Time is got a heaper flewjus mixt up wid it. You think it's a-standin' still, but all de time it's des a-cally-hootin', an' a-humpin' an' a-totin' de mail. You can't hear de engine, but dey's one dar. *Returns,* p. 83.

Comet: Dis yer stair [star] w'at shows up 'fo' day wid 'er back hair down . . . She's a sight mon! She look lak she done drap loose fum some'rs en lef' a streak er fier behime 'er ez big ez er omlybus en long ez a freight train; en honey, she's des a-collyhootin'. *Friends,* p:

262. He call out yo' name mo' dan once, an' he put some langwidge 'roun' it dat 'ud burn a hole in my tongue, ef I wuz ter say it. *Returns,* p. 89.
He des waller'd in fat; he wuz too fat to keep de flies off'n himself. *Friends,* p. 15.

The pictorial language always arrested the attention of the little boy to whom Uncle Remus told the stories, and it continues to charm those who read them. Sometimes the words have no meaning but are used as Harris says because of their sonorousness. A few examples will illustrate this phase:

De leafs dey'd go swishy-swushy; splushy-spilshy. *Nights,* p. 4.
He sniffle an' snuffle. *Tar-Baby,* p. 41.

She grinned a grin, an' she clucked a cluck
Wid Law's a-massy! What luck! What luck!
Tar Baby, p. 93.

She flung a flutter. *Tar-Baby,* p. 94.
Brer Buzzud come sailin' all 'roun' wid dat 'Boo, boo, boo, my filler-mer-doo.' *Nights,* p. 122.
He sneeze a snoze and wheeze a whoze. *Told By,* p. 219.
Dis look so pleezy-plozzy. *Nights,* p. 288.
Brer B'ar got his tail broke off smick-smack-smoove. *Nights,* p. 115.
He ain't so much as bubble a bubble. *Told By,* p. 219.
I'm a ginin' you de fatal fack. *Nights,* p. 211.
In dar whar de king's doin' his kingin'. *Returns,* p. 100.

Some of the expressions depend for their interest upon *invented* or *mistaken* words. Examples of invented words are:

He be dog his cats ef he don't *slorate* ole Brer Rabbit. *Nights,* p. 9.
Dey *jower'd* awhile. *Returns,* p. 90.
He look mighty *solumcolly.* *Told By,* p. 178.

Make him feel mighty *umble-come-tumble. Friends,* p. 55.

Take notice er all dish yer kinder *jugglements* en gwines on. *Nights,* p. 269.

Dey better quit der *'havishness* an' l'arn how ter don't. *Friends,* p. 114.

Ef I ain't mighty much mistooken, he done gone an' got a case er *highstericks. Told By,* p. 142.

An' de *fergiven* name . . . wuz Remus. *S. and S.,* p. 219.

I'd a gouged out his *goozle* fust. *Returns,* p. 113.

Ef you'll wet yo' thumb an' turn back in yo' min' 'twon't be hard fer you ter *reckermember. Returns,* p. 110.

Brer Coon feel like a nat'al-born *Slink. Nights,* p. 112.

You is *high-primin'* 'roun' des lak you done had mo' supper dan de king er *philanders. Nights,* p. 113.

Dey wisht mighty strong dat der *cants* wuz *coulds. Tar-Baby,* p. 6.

Examples of mistaken words (misspelled or the use of one part of speech for another):

An' den he *smole* one er deze here lopsided smiles. *Told By,* p. 271.

Ef you think I got time fer ter stop right short off en *stribbit* [distribute] out all I knows, you er mighty much mistaken. *Nights,* p. 214.

Ef she'd 'a' know'd at fust what she know at last, she'd take two long thinks an' a mighty big *thunk,* 'fo' she'd marry anybody in de roun' worl'. *Returns,* p. 95.

I ain't gwine inter court an' make no *affledave* on it. *Told By,* p. 211.

I'm a flingin' de *essent* er de trufe at you. *Friends,* p. 261.

De nighes' way out'n dis *diffikil. Nights,* p. 106.

So mighty *disaccomerdatin'. Nights,* p. 106.

You got de whole sidewalk for a *flatform* [platform]. *S. and S.,* p. 283.

Preachers des gits up in dese *pulypits*. *Friends*, p. 375.
Rabbit kin have his *choosement*. *Returns*, p. 96.
Know his will an' *desirements*. *Returns*, p. 96.
Brer Fox say he sorter *middlin'* peart, en Brer Rabbit say he sorter betwix' '*My gracious!*', and '*Thank gracious!*'. *Friends*, p. 124.

A few of the sayings may be classified as Wellerisms—a special type of proverb which involves a comparison such as Mr. Sam Weller of *Pickwick Papers* used to enjoy making. "The favorite Wellerism in New York State undoubtedly is, 'Every man to his taste, as the Irishman said when he kissed the cow'." [7]

Two examples from the Uncle Remus book are:

> An' a mighty good reason—but dat's a tale,
> Ez de possum said ter de slippery rail.
> *Tar-Baby*, p. 1.
>
> You know w'at de jay-bird say ter der squinch owl!
> 'I'm sickly but sassy.' *Nights*, p. 298.

This may be compared to such present-day nonsensical sayings of the folk as:

> What did the mayonnaise say to the ice-box?
> 'Close the door, I'm dressing.'

Scattered through the books are sayings whose humor derives from play on words such as:

> "What you say yo' name might be?"
> "Wm. Henry Haddem."
> "Haddem had um, and now he ain't got um."
> *Friends*, p. 268.

Many of the philosophical folks sayings are proverbial:
Folks is folks en creeturs is creeturs, en you can't make um needer mo' ner less. You er what you is, en you can't be no is-er; I'm what I am, en I can't be no am-er.[8] It all done been fix, en I ain't see nobody yit what kin unfix it. *Friends*, p. 69.

You des got ter lean back en make 'lowances fer all sorts er folks. You got ter 'low fer dem dat knows too much, same ez dem w'at knows too little. *Nights,* p. 250.

A heap er sayin's en a heap er doin's in dis roun' worl' got ter be tuck on trus'. You got yo' sayin's, I got mine; you got yo' knowin's, en I got mine. *Nights,* p. 250.

I ain't never see no polergy [apology] what wuz poultice er plarster nuff fer ter swaje [assuage] a swellin' er kyo [cure] a bruise. Now you kin des keep dat in yo' min' en git sorry fo' you hurt anybody. I been takin' notice deze many long years dat 'Didn't-go-to-do-it' is de ve'y chap what do it all. *Friends,* p. 85.

I done fin' out in my time dat dey don't nothin' pay like perliteness, speshually ef she's ginnywine. *Told By,* p. 38.

Dey ain't no fun in bein' a king, kaze yo' time ain't yo' own, an' you can't turn 'roun' widout skinnin' yo' shins on some by-law er nother. *Told By,* p. 116.

When folks ain't got much ter do, an' little er nothin' fer ter talk 'bout, dey'll soon git ter braggin'. *Told By,* p. 91.

You gotter travel wid a circus 'fo' you gits away wid me. *S. and S.,* p. 234.

You dunner how 'tis dat dat ar acorn in yo' han' is got a great big oak tree in it. Dey got ter be a startin' place. Ef trees wuz ter start out trees, you'd see a monstus upsettin' all aroun'. *Friends,* p. 42.

Yasser, you can't please eve'ybody. Ef youer hangin' um, er makin' a seine, or tellin' a tale, somebody er sump'n will say, 'tain't de right thing. *Returns,* p. 57.

'Zease an' trouble an' one thing an' an'er is all de time makin' de 'rouns, en de places where folks live at. *Returns,* p. 117.

Folks ain't got no business mockin' de way creeturs does. Dey er bound ter git cotch up wid, en right den dey er in deep trouble. Creeturs kin take what ain' dern, en tell fibs, en dey don't no harm come fum it; but when folks tries it, dey er bleedz to come to some bad end. *Friends*, p. 166.

In Harris's collection of proverbs in *Uncle Remus: His Songs and His Sayings*,[9] one can follow the general classifications already used in this chapter for grouping some of the maxims. There are several in the general group of wisdom which are proverbs of warning:

Ole man Know-All died last year.
Save de pacin' mar' fer Sunday.
Crow en corn can't grow in de same fiel'.
Dem w'at knows too much sleeps under de ash-hopper.
Pullet can't roost too high for de owl.
Don't fling away de empty wallet.
Black-snake know de way ter de hin nes'.
Licker talks mighty loud w'en it git loose fum de jug.
De proudness un a man don't count w'en he fine a wum.
You may know de way, but batter keep yo' eyes on de seven stairs [stars].
You kin hide de fier, but w'at you gwine do wid de smoke?
Ter-morrer may be de carridge-driver's day for ploughin'.
De pig dat runs off wid de year er corn gits little mo' den de cob.
Watch out w'en you'er gitting all you want. Fattenin' hogs ain't in luck.

Some treat of *industry and thrift*:

Dram ain't good twel you git it.
Rails split 'fo' bre'kfus' 'll season de dinner.
Mighty po' bee dat don't make mo' honey dan he want.
Kwishins [cushions] on mule's foots done gone out er fashion.
Bline hoss don't fall w'en he follers de bit.
Looks won't do ter split rails wid.
Nigger dat gets hurt wukkin oughter show de skyars

[scars].
Sleepin' in de fence-corner don't fetch Christmus in de kitchen.

Many show ironical or cynical observation:

Tattlin' 'oman can't make de bread rise.
Hog dunner w'ich part un 'im 'll season de turnip salad.
Winter grape sour, whedder you kin reach 'im or not.
Dogs don't bite at the front gate.
Hongry nigger won't w'ar his maul out.
Rooster makes mo' racket dan de hin w'at lay de aig.
Nigger wid a pocket-hancher better be looked atter.
All de buzzards in de settlement 'll come to de gray mule's funer'l.
Hit's mighty deaf nigger dat don't hear de dinner horn.
Ha'nts don't bodder longer hones' folks, but you better go 'roun' de grave-yard.
'Twix de bug en de bee-martin 'tain't hard ter tell w'ich gwineter git kotch.

A few are for special occasions:

Don't rain eve'ytime de pig squeal.
Colt in de barley patch kick high.
Empty smoke-house makes de pullet holler.

The plantation and the conditions which produced the proverbs of Uncle Remus are gone, but the proverbial language of the Negro goes on. The artistic poetic impulse, the gift of condensation, and above all the vivid imagery and pictorial language are continually in the making, and may yet be heard on the street corner, in the village store, on the college campus, on the farm, or on the avenue. To interested searchers in a field largely untrodden such collecting should yield a rich harvest.

IX

DIALECT

"De ins en de outs er dat kinder talk all come ter de same p'int in my min'."—Nights with Uncle Remus.

JOEL CHANDLER HARRIS STANDS AMONG THE GREATEST writers of dialect in the world. He developed to the utmost the gift of recording the speech of the plantation Negro. So accurately and faithfully has he reproduced the dialect that persons in Georgia who have heard the speech of some of the ante-bellum Negroes can almost hear them speaking, through Uncle Remus. In many sections of the country people who were not familiar with his biography thought he was a Negro. Once when he was visiting in New Orleans a large number of citizens turned out to meet him, and when he appeared there were whispers throughout the crowd, "Look, he's white."

There is another legend told in this same connection. Eugene Fields, who was Harris's friend and whom he greatly admired, started a fantastic story about Harris's birth and early life which was circulated in a large number of newspapers. At first it amused Harris since he too was a great jokester. But when Field carried the joke a little further and said that the "son of missionary parents"—hence the master of dialect—was the richest author in America, and letters of solicitation began coming in from all sources, Harris thought the jest had gone beyond the funny stage.

One of the versions of the tale was:

> Joel Chandler Harris, the Southern dialetician and *litterateur,* sails for Africa in December, it being his purpose to revisit the little coast town of Joel, where he was born of missionary parents January 13, 1842. Mr. Harris lost a leg in the battle of Lookout Mountain. His career has been full of incidents.[1]

Another version was:

> Joel C. Harris has had a strangely romantic career. His father was a missionary, and it was at the small town of Booghia, on the South Coast of Africa, that Joel was born. He was educated by his father and acquired a wonderful acquaintance with foreign languages. He is an adept Sanskrit scholar and is deeply versed in Hebraic and Buddhist literature. The sweetly quaint legends of Indian and Judean mythology have found their way into his simple Southern tales, and the spirit of his philosophy is identical with the teachings of Moses and Buddha.[2]

Since the mastery of the dialect is one of Harris's notable appeals, his own statements with regard to the dialect are revealing. In the Introduction to the first Remus book he stated:

> . . . my purpose has been to preserve the legends themselves in their original simplicity, and to wed them permanently to the quaint dialect—if, indeed, it can be called a dialect—through the medium of which they have become a part of the domestic history of every Southern family. . . . The dialect, it will be observed, is wholly different from that of the Hon. Pompey Smash and his literary descendants, and different also from the intolerable misrepresentations of the minstrel stage, but it is at least phonetically genuine. Nevertheless, if the language of Uncle Remus fails to give vivid hints of the really poetic imagination of the negro; if it fails to embody the quaint and homely humor which was his most prominent characteristic; if it

does not suggest a certain picturesque sensitiveness—a curious exaltation of mind and temperament not to be defined by words—then I have reproduced the form of the dialect merely, and not the essence, and my attempt may be counted a failure.[3]

He also comments on the difference between the dialect of the legends included in *Uncle Remus: His Songs and His Sayings* and that of the character sketches in the same book. Slight as it is, he states that it "marks the modifications which the speech of the negro has undergone even where education has played no part in reforming it. Indeed, save in the remote country districts, the dialect of the legends has nearly disappeared."[4]

In *Nights with Uncle Remus* (1883) he wrote:

In the Introduction to the first volume of Uncle Remus, a lame apology was made for inflicting a book of dialect upon the public. Perhaps a similar apology should be made here; but the discriminating reader does not need to be told that it would be impossible to separate these stories from the idiom in which they have been recited for generations. The dialect is a part of the legends themselves, and to present them in any other way would be to rob them of everything that gives them vitality.[5]

Included in the collection of stories in *Nights* are some which were sent Mr. Harris from friends who lived on the rice plantations and Sea Islands. These are related by Daddy Jack, whose speech is Gullah dialect. Harris says of the Gullah, "though it may seem at first glance to be more difficult than that of Uncle Remus, it is in reality, simpler and more direct," but even Georgians are not likely to agree.

As to the meaning of the word *Gullah* we have an explanation published late in the nineteenth century:

"Gullah" is very probably a corruption of Angola, a country of West Africa, shortened to Gola, and a part of Lower Guinea, from which a great many negroes were brought to this country in the days of the slave trade. I remember hearing the old plantation negroes before the war speak of one as a "Guinea nigger." In Appleton's "New American Cyclopedia," the Guinea negroes are described as "black and having thick lips and flat noses," and the Angola or "Gullah" negroes as having "few of the negro peculiarities of form and feature. They are brown in color." These differences between negroes in the country have been often noticed and remarked upon frequently, the explanation of which differences is that the "thick lips" and "flat noses" point to Ashantee and Dahomey as the places from which their ancestors were brought and the "brown color" and features, more like the European in some negroes, very different from the Guineas, point to Angola or "Gullah," as the country from which their ancestors came.

If before the war a rice field negro, a true blue Gullah, was hurried from his eating to his work, he was most sure to be heard mumbling to himself: 'Dis berry hahd, des buckra ent gib me time to nyam me bittle!' [This is very hard these white men won't give me time to eat my victuals].[6]

The same author, writing on incidents of the old plantation, calls attention to the history of the word nyam. He wrote:

The word Nyam, meaning a sweet potato, is very likely a Spanish word, as in all probability the Spaniards introduced into this country the sweet as well as the Irish potato. "Nyam tetter" was always the way the Gullah negro called sweet potatoes. But why did he say "nyam" for "eat"? Well, here is the history in the word, nyam. Sweet potatoes, which he called "nyam" for "yam tetter" was his chief eating, given to him for his 'lowance', his main stand by, and hence came to signify eating itself.[7]

Another commentator on the Gullah dialect, C. Alphonso Smith, calls attention to the fact that "It has given us . . . the only pure African word still current in negro speech, the word *buckra,* meaning *boss* or *overseer.*"[8]

The only Uncle Remus book in which Harris employs Gullah is *Nights,* in which he comments at length upon its use as employed by Daddy Jack:

The dialect of Daddy Jack . . . is the negro dialect in its most primitive state—the "Gullah" talk of some of the negroes on the Sea Islands, being merely a confused and untranslatable mixture of English and African words. In the introductory notes to "Slave Songs of the United States" [1867], may be found an exposition of Daddy Jack's dialect as complete as any that can be given here. A key to the dialect may be given very briefly. The vocabulary is not an extensive one—more depending upon the manner, the form of expression, and the inflection, than upon the words employed. It is thus an admirable vehicle for story-telling. It recognizes no gender, and scorns the use of plural number except accidentally. "E" stands for "he" "she" or "it", and "dem" may allude to one thing or may include a thousand. The dialect is laconic and yet rambling, full of repetitions, and abounding in curious elisions, that give an unexpected quaintness to the simplest statements. A glance at the following vocabulary will enable the reader to understand Daddy Jack's dialect perfectly, though allowance must be made for inversions and elisions.

B'er, brother.
Beer, bear.
Bittle, victuals.
Bre't, breath.
Buckra, white man, overseer, boss.
Churrah, churray, spill, splash.
Da, the, that.
Dey, there.
Dey-dey, here, down there, right here.
Enty, ain't he? an exclamation of astonishment or assent.
Gwan, going.
Leaf, leave.
Lif, live.
Lil, lil-a, or *lilly,* little.
Lun, learn.
Mek, make.
Neat', or *nead,* underneath, beneath.
Oona, you, all of you.
Sem, same.
Shum, see them, saw them.
Tam, time.
'Tan', stand.

Tankee, thanks, thank you.
Tark, or *tahlk,* talk.
Teer, tear.
Tek, take.
T'ink, or *t'ought,* think, thought.
T'row, throw.
Titty, or *titter,* sissy, sister.
Trute, truth.
Turrer, or *tarrah,* the other.
Tusty, thirsty.
Urrer, other.
Wey, where.
Wun, when.
Wut, what.
Y'et, or *ut,* earth.
Yeddy, or *yerry,* heard, hear.
Yent, *ain't,* isn't.

The trick of adding a vowel to sound words is not unpleasing to the ear. Thus: "I bin-a wait fer you; come-a ring-a dem bell. Wut mek-a (or mekky) you stay so?" "Yeddy", "yerry", and probably "churry" are the result of this—heard-a, yeard-a, yeddy; hear-a, year-a, yerry; chur-a, churray. When "eye" is written "y-eye", it is to be pronounced "yi." In such words as "back", "ax", *a* has the sound of *ah.* They are written "bahk", "ahx".[9]

In *Friends,* Harris's third Uncle Remus book, he is still conscious of the use of dialect, and feels the necessity for remarks concerning it. Here he said:

Naturally, these stories are written in what is called negro dialect. It seemed to be unavoidable. I sympathize deeply and heartily with the protest that has been made against the abuse of dialect. It is painful, indeed, when the form of the lingo trails on the earth, and the thought flies in the air. I had intended to apologize for the plantation dialect, but a valued correspondent in "The Flatwoods" assures me that "old man Chaucer was one of the earliest dialect writers," and I have recently seen (in the "New York Independent") an essay by Professor March, in which there is a perfectly serious effort to rival the phonetics employed by Uncle Remus.

The student of English, if he be willing to search so near the ground, will find matter to interest him in the homely dialect of Uncle Remus, and if his intentions run towards philological investigations, he will pause before he has gone far and ask himself whether this negro dialect is what it purports to be, or whether it is not simply the language of the white people of three hundred years ago twisted and modified a little to fit the lingual peculiarities of the negro. Dozens of words, such as "*hit* for *it*, *ax* for *ask*, *whiles* for *wiles*, and *heap* for a large number of people, will open before him the whole field of the philology of the English tongue. He will discover that, when Uncle Remus tells the little boy that he has a "monstus weakness fer cake what's got *reezins* in it," the pronunciation of *reezins* uncovers and rescues from oblivion Shakespeare's pun on *raisins*, where Falstaff tells the Prince, "If reasons were as plentiful as blackberries, I would give no man a reason on compulsion." [10]

The Uncle Remus dialect is characterized by the adaptation of existing English words as well as the addition of words (many of which seem nonsensical) for the pictorial effect, the euphony, and the delight which the Negro has for "big words" (that is, many-syllabled words) with which he likes to astound his audience. Though the language spoken by Uncle Remus represents that of Middle Georgia, C. Alphonso Smith points out that some of the words are also found in the dialect of Virginia; Professor Smith explains this on the grounds that Uncle Remus admits that he "come from Ferginny." Among the words common to both sections are: seegyar and gyardin. Certain characteristics are noted by Professor Smith: the plurals of all nouns tend to become regular, as foots, toofies, gooses; *which* takes the place of the relative pronoun *who;* there is the tendency to add the "s" to all forms of the verb as *I makes.*[11]

Harris greatly enjoyed writing the rural dialect when it was integral part of character. In regard to the Negro dialect, he wrote to the editor of *Scribner's Magazine,* in November, 1898: "I am very fond of writing this dialect

. . . it gives a new coloring to statement, and allows of a swift shading in narrative that can be reached in literary English only in the most painful and roundabout way." He insisted, however, that to write dialect merely for itself was meaningless: "In all dialects the thought exactly fits the expression—the idea is as homely as the words—and any attempt to reproduce a dialect must recognize this fact or be pronounced a failure." [12]

Throughout his books his dialect is the best to be found anywhere; it is convincing to the very smallest phrase. It is the belief of some critics that it was mainly because of his mastery of the vernacular that he achieved his triumph. Walter H. Page wrote in 1881: "I have Mr. Harris's own word for it that he can *think* in the negro dialect. He could translate even Emerson, perhaps Bronson Alcott, in it, as well as he can tell the adventures of Brer Rabbit." [13]

Julia Collier Harris in an article, "Uncle Remus at Home and Abroad" comments upon two anglicized versions of some of the stories and expresses the opinion that Harris would never have been pleased by the deletion of the dialect. She wrote: "Naturally, he would never have given his permission to delete the dialect, no matter what compensation had been offered him." [14]

Mrs. Thaddeus Horton describes a scene upon the occasion of Andrew Carnegie's visit to Harris at Snap-Bean Farm, Harris's home, and a portion of the dialogue which referred to Harris's use of dialect:

> There they sat together: the builder of libraries, and the contributor to libraries. Both were farmers and showed it in their dress; both wore old clothes, old shoes, and big hats.
>
> "Well, well," said the genial millionaire Scotsman; "How are you?"
>
> "Po'ly," said Uncle Remus, still chuckling.
>
> "What's the matter?" asked Mr. Carnegie anxiously as he viewed the rotund form and beaming face before him.
>
> "I'm thinking of applying to you for a pension," said Uncle Remus. "I'm about to be cut out of an honest living."

"How's that?" said Mr. Carnegie?

"It's this phonetic spelling you've started."

"Why bless you, man, I'm just doing it in compliment to you to show you how much I like your spelling."

"That's the trouble," chuckled Uncle Remus. "When the people see how easy it is. I'm afraid everyone will take to writing dialect." [15]

However, his fears were ungrounded, for there was no one in his day, nor has there been one since who has found the writing of the type of dialect with which he enriched literature "easy."

Thomas Nelson Page, himself an adept in the use of Negro dialect, writing in the "Book-Buyer," December, 1895, concerning Harris's gift of writing in dialect said: "No man who has ever written has known one-tenth part about the negro that Mr. Harris knows, and for those who hereafter shall wish to find not merely words, but the real language of the negro of that section, and the habits of all American negroes of the old time, his works will prove the best thesaurus." [16]

X

SONGS

You sang not deeds of heroes or of kings;
No chant of bloody war, no exulting paean
Of arms-won triumph; but your humble strings
  You touched in chord with music empyrean.
You sang far better than you knew; the songs
That for your listeners' hungry hearts sufficed
Still live,—but more than this to you belongs:
  You sang a race from wood and stone to Christ.

"O Black and Unknown Bards"
—James Weldon Johnson.

THE VERY YEAR THAT SAW THE PUBLICATION OF *Uncle Remus: His Songs and His Sayings* was that in which another Georgian, Sidney Lanier, brought out an important treatise, *The Science of English Verse.* It is interesting to note that their theories coincide. Statements interpolated in several Introductions to Harris's Uncle Remus books show that he had given a good deal of thought and time to the study of prosody.

In the Introduction to the first Uncle Remus book, which contained nine songs, Harris wrote:

As to the songs, the reader is warned that it will be found difficult to make them conform to the ordinary rules of versification, nor is it intended that they should so conform. They are written, and are intended to be read, solely with reference to the regular and invariable recurrence of the caesura, as, for instance, the first stanza of the Revival Hymn:

"Oh, whar | shill we go | w'en de great | day comes |
Wid de blow | in 'er de trumpits | en de bang | in
'er de drums |
How man | y po' sin | ners'll be kotch'd | out late
En fine | no latch | ter de gold | en gate | "

In other words, the songs depend for their melody and rhythm upon the musical quality of *time*, and not upon long or short, accented syllables. I am persuaded that this fact led Mr. Sidney Lanier, who is thoroughly familiar with the metrical peculiarities of negro songs, into the exhaustive investigation which has resulted in his scholarly treatise on The Science of English Verse.[1]

In the Introduction to *Tar-Baby and Other Rhymes*, in giving his reason for the version of the Tar-Baby story in rhyme, Harris makes further comment on meter.

Those who care for the narratives themselves will no doubt overlook the somewhat monotonous character of the verse. When Uncle Remus sets himself to produce new stories in a form that would seem to be alien to his methods, it is inevitable that his methods should move along the line of least resistance which is the iambic four-beat movement, the simplest form of narrative verse. Under the circumstances, and in view of his environment, it is natural that he should pay small attention to the misleading rules of the professors of prosody, who seem to have not the slightest notion of the science of English verse. His instinctive love of melody, and his appreciation of the simplest rhythmical movement would lead him to ignore syllables and accent and to depend wholly on the time-movement that is inseparable from English verse.[2]

RELIGIOUS SONGS

Of the twenty-six songs included in the Uncle Remus books, eight are religious—spirituals or hymns. Spirituals are folk music orally transmitted or developed communally. Just how accurate Harris has been in recording the songs one is unable to say. There are some instances where he states that they have been literally transcribed; in other cases, he makes no such notations. Nevertheless, as expressions of folk experiences with the flavor and tang of the life in a period which was difficult, and from which the Negro looked toward a better day, they are important representations. The religious songs in the eight volumes are:

1. "Revival Hymn" (*S. and S.*, p. 155). Four eight-line stanzas.
2. "Camp-Meeting Song" (*S. and S.*, p. 156). Four eight-line stanzas.
3. "A Plantation Chant" (*S. and S.*, p. 166). Three twelve-line stanzas.
4. "De Big Bethel Church" (*S. and S.*, p. 169). Four ten-line stanzas.
5. "Time Goes By Turns" (*S. and S.*, p. 170). Seven four-line stanzas.
6. "Dem Lam's A-Cryin' " (*Friends*, p. 199). Six four-line stanzas.
7. "Come Along, True Believer!" (*Friends*, p. 204). Three twelve-line stanzas.
8. "Ring Dem Charmin' Bells" (*Friends*, p. 210). Five nine-line stanzas.

Most of the songs show trials of this life and rejoicing at the thought of heaven. Some few give moral exhortations or admonitions to sinners. Although some of the pictorial descriptions border on the humorous and some of the rhythms are lively, these spirituals are deeply serious and earnest.

In the "Revival Hymn" there is exultation in the belief that the great day is coming "Wid de blowin' er de trumpits en de bangin' er de drums." Sinners are warned against being "kotched out late en fin' no latch ter de golden gate." Sin is "ez sharp ez a bamboo brier." Old Satan is "loose en a-bummin'." The final plea is,

> Fight de battles er de Lord, fight soon and fight late
> En you'll allers fin' a latch ter de golden gate.

"Camp-Meeting Song" is a prayer song with other factors entering. There is first the request that the "Lord 'member dese chillun in de mornin'." It was this ray of hope—that tomorrow things would be better—that, Alain Locke remarks, "preserved the emotional sanity of the Negro and kept his spirit somewhat above the fate of his body." [3] Sinners are urged to leave the scoffing crowd and join the Christians. The hand of redemption is held out —a patient hand it is, but the days are few and all should be looking toward the "green hills of grace."

> Oh, you allers will be wrong
> Twel you choose ter belong
> Ter de Marster w'at's a-comin' in de mornin'!

This song has authentic imagery, but the twelve-line stanza is more elaborate than we expect to find in folk spirituals.

Of "A Plantation Chant" and one secular song Harris wrote: "If these are adaptations from songs the negroes have caught from the whites, their origin is very remote. I have transcribed them literally, and I regard them in the highest degree characteristic." [4] The song expresses dissatisfaction with this world, "I don't wanter stay yer no longer." It employs a series of dates, beginning:

> Hit's eighteen hunder'd forty-en-fo',
> Christ done open dat He'v'mly do'—

and progresses by two years in each stanza until in the last:

> Hit's eighteen hunder'd forty-en-ten,
> Christ is de mo'ner's onliest fr'en'—
> An' I don't wanter stay yer no longer;
> Hit's eighteen hunder'd forty-en-'lev'm,
> Christ'll be at de do' w'en we all git ter Hev'm—
> An' I don't wanter stay yer no longer.

The use of dates suggests a railroad song about Irish workers probably familiar to the Negroes and Harris. In John and Alan Lomax's version, this begins,

> In eighteen hundred and forty-wan
> I put me cord'roy breeches on, . . . [5]

"De Big Bethel Church" is a song of praise for the power of this particular church. In Georgia the name is generally associated with the A. M. E. (African Methodist Episcopal) Church; in every city of a certain population where there is a branch of this denomination, there is a Big Bethel Church. So potent is its influence that:

> Ef a sinner git loose fum enny udder chu'ch,
> De Big Bethel chu'ch will fin' um.

The song further points out the jubilance of the social contact.

> Hit's good ter be dere, en it's sweet ter be dere,
> Wid de sisterin' all aroun' you—

The fervor and ecstasy is such that there is no room for weeping and doubting. The congregation is filled with entrancing joy when a large number of sinners are converted,

> En it look like Gaberl gwine ter rack up en blow
> En set dem heav'm bells ter ringin'!

This is one of the four Harris songs in which bells are mentioned—an example of his use of imagery found in authentic spirituals. The four-line stanza suggests in rhythm a camp-meeting hymn.

"Time Goes by Turns" is a dramatic expression of the "rassle 'twix de Good en de Bad." There is an element of narrative balladry here. Bad come "i'on-clad" and seems as if she will win;

> But des todes de las' Good gits de knee-lock,
> En dey draps ter de ground-kerflop!
> Good had de inturn, en he stan' like a rock,
> En he bleedzd fer ter be on top.

So it is with every phase of life; there is bad mixed with the good. The moral is, therefore,

Hump yo'se'f ter de load en fergit de distress,
  En dem w'at stan's by ter scoff,
Fer de harder de pullin', de longer de res',
  En de bigger de feed in de troff.[6]

"Dem Lam's A-Cryin' " has the familiar theme of many of the spirituals, the most popular of which is perhaps "Listen to de Lambs." Though this does not re-tell a Bible story, it does mention two Biblical characters, Paul and Silas, also familiar in spirituals. Jesus is referred to as the "Good Shepherd" who has the power to make one's heart rejoice.

"Ring Dem Charmin' Bells" is another of the "Bell Songs". It pictures the trials here below—"Hit's a Road full er faintin' spells"; the road is long, full of dust, but some day you will hear "dem charmin' bells". This is one of the numerous songs in which the River Jordan is mentioned.[7]

W'en de night get dark en col',
En you year dat Jerdun roll,
  Dat de place whar John befells;

With regard to the last line in the above quotation Harris explains, "This is what befell St. John." He also calls attention to other songs in which the River Jordan is mentioned, and he says: "It may be well to state in this connection that this attempt to render the spirit of a very quaint song should not be confounded with 'Roll Jordan Roll', the music of which has been preserved with wonderful success by the late Mrs. Lucy McKim Garrison, nor with another song with the same refrain. The rolling of Jordan and the ringing of the charming bells are heard in a dozen negro songs.[8]

WORK SONGS

In Africa, the Negro had sung to the rhythm as he worked, and he continued this rhythmic labor in America. There are five songs in the Uncle Remus Series of this type:

1. "Corn-Shucking Song" (*Tar-Baby*, p. 142).
2. "Corn-Shucking Song" (*Friends*, p. 201).
3. "The Plough Hand's Song" (*Friends*, p. 193).
4. "Oh, July! Dis Long Time!" (*Friends*, p. 202).
5. "Hog-Feeder's Song" (*Friends*, p. 212).

"Corn-Shucking Song" (*Tar-Baby*) has intricate use of refrain-lines such as "Hey O! Hi O! Up'n down de Bango." It gives a picture of daybreak and the necessity for men hastening to work. As in many of the songs, there is a large number of references to animals; here are mentioned the red calf, squinch owl, the roan mule, Mr. Rabbit, Fox.

To the "Corn-Shucking Song" (*Friends*) Harris appended the following note; "A rail was placed in the middle of the corn-pile, at the bottom. The shuckers were divided into competing gangs, and there was a rivalry as to which side should reach the rail first. Hence the song."[9] There is also a refrain here:

Oh row, row, row! who laid dat rail?
Rinktum, ranktum, laid dat rail!
Show me the nigger dat laid dat rail
Oh, row, row, row! who laid dat rail?

The refrain varies. The first and last stanzas are the same, but at the conclusion of the second stanza the words are:

Big-foot nigger dat laid dat rail!
Oh row, row, row! who laid dat rail?
Rinktum, ranktum, laid dat rail!

The refrain choruses in "The Plough-Hands' Song"[10] differ from the refrains in most of the other songs; "Dat sun's a-slantin' " appears three times in each stanza, but at the end of each stanza there is a "refrain chorus":

Good-night, Mr. Killdee! I wish you mighty well
—Mr. Killdee! I wish you mighty well!
I wish you mighty well!

Harris's explanation of the refrain chorus is: "The italics serve to mark what may be called the refrain choruses. The variable nature of these gives unexpected coloring, not to say humor to the songs in which they occur. Any typographical arrangement of these choruses must be, in the very nature of things, awkward and ineffective." [11]

Just as one of the Corn-Shucking Songs presented pictorially the morning scene on the plantation, "The Plough-Hands' Song" reveals such a scene in the evening. The workers have been watching the sun; they are joyous as the time approaches for it to set:

Dat sun's a-slantin';
Dat sun's a-slantin' en slippin' down still!
Den sing it out, Primus! des holler en bawl,
En w'ilst we er strippin' dese mules fer de stall,
Let de gals ketch de soun' er de plantashun call;
Oh, it's good-night ladies! my love unter you all,
—Ladies! my love unter you all!
—My love unter you all!

"Oh, July! Dis Long Time!" is dated at Putnam County, Georgia, 1858. This would seem to give evidence that Harris collected it at this time and possibly rendered it just as he heard it. However, one comment is: "J. A. Macon and Joel Chandler Harris collected several slave songs, but in rendering them to the public, they forced them into patterns of standard versifying." [12] The song has four stanzas, in each of which an animal is mentioned, and the theme seems to be summed up in the line "En yit Mr. Coon gits cotch at last." So the Rabbit, though clever, finally lands in the pot; the Fox gets over ground but is always run down; Mr. Mink though "slicker dan sin" will lose his skin. The refrain chorus consists of four lines:

Oh, July! Mighty wrong time!
Mighty wrong time! Oh, July!
Oh, July! Mighty long time!
Mighty long time! Oh, July!

In a note at the conclusion of the song, Harris wrote:

This refrain chorus belongs to a dozen different songs. Its meaning must be taken literally. July is a long time, a hot time, and a strong time to those who work in the sun.[13]

Perhaps the best exposition of "The Hog-Feeder's Song" is that given by Harris in *On the Plantation*:

Harbert turned his attention to calling his hogs, and the way he did this was . . . interesting to Joe [Harris]. . . . He had a voice of wonderful strength and power, as penetrating and as melodious as the notes of a cornet. On a still day when there was little moisture in the air, Harbert could make himself heard two miles. The range over which the hogs roamed was at least a mile and a half from the pen. In calling them the negro broke into song. It was only the refrain that the distant hogs could hear, but as it went echoing over the hills and valleys it seemed to be the very essence of melody.[14]

The song was something like this:

Hog-Feeder's Song

Oh, rise up, my ladies, lissen unter me,
Gwoop! Gwoop! Gee-woop! Goo-whee!
I'm a-gwine dis night fer ter knock along er you.
Gwoop! Gwoop! Gee-woop! Goo-whoo!
Pig-goo! Pig-gee! Gee-o-whee!

The song is a medley consisting of an address to the ladies, comment on the stars, observation on the sense of the old sow, and admonition to a fat pig to stay close because he will "taste mighty good in a barbecue." The refrain, a hog-call, differs from stanza to stanza.

LOVE SONGS

The three love songs collected by Harris are:

1. "Oh, Gimme De Gal!" (*Friends*, p. 196).

2. "A Negro Love Song" (*Friends*, p. 206).
3. "My Honey, My Love" (*Friends*, p. 215).

"Oh, Gimme De Gal!" is a curious mixture of things, people, and events—the boss squalls to the boys not to bother the jug in the spring; the Negroes "don't cut no shine" when the boss looks through the fence; the little bird flutters when the big speckle hawk sails up in the pine tree; the overseer leans his chin on the fence and listens to the cotton-choppers sing. The essence of the song they sing is:

Don't nobody bodder dat sway-back gal
W'at wrop up 'er ha'r wid a string!

The last stanza is:

Oh, de strappin' black gal, de big greasy gal!
She kyar herse'f mighty fine!
How de boys gwineter foller along in de row,
A-waitin' fer ter ketch her sign?
De boss mighty close, yit I study en I wish—
En I wish dat big gal 'uz mine! [15]

Paul Laurence Dunbar's "Love Song" has a refrain similar to "A Negro Love Song"; in Dunbar's it is "Jump Back! Honey, Jump Back!"; here it is "Hey my Lily! go down de road!" In each stanza of Harris's song the lover asks that his walking cane be handed him, so that he can call to see his girl and they will walk down the lane. As in many of the other songs there are references to nature —"Sun gone down en de moon done showed", "Hit's wet on de grass whar de jew bin po'd." Thomas W. Talley makes the observation, "The Negro communed with Nature and she gave him Rhymes for amusement." [16] The rabbit, kildee, owl, and chicken are mentioned. In the last stanza there is also a bit of wisdom:

One man lose w'at n'er man gain.

The first appearance of "My Honey, My Love" is in *Nights with Uncle Remus*. It is supposed to be sung at the wedding feast after the marriage of 'Tildy and Daddy

Jack. Harris admitted that when the words were put in print they seemed meaningless, but he stated that if one could hear the rich melody one would forget that words were important. Evidently, Daddy Jack was going to carry 'Tildy back to his home near the coast and she was saying farewell to her former associates and friends.

Hit's a Mighty fur ways up de Far-well Lane,
My honey, my love!

There are five stanzas; each has the refrain,

My honey, my love, my heart's delight—
My honey, my love!

The song might have been a dance song, for one line is Tu'n lef', tu'n right, we'll dance all night.

Talley makes a reference to a type of rhymes which he calls the Social Instinct type—an expression of primitive courtship, "the crude call of one heart and the crude response of another heart." It is interesting to note that the expression "Honey love" of Harris's song also occurs in one of the lines of "Antebellum Courtship Inquiry":

(He) —"Is you a flyin' lark, or a settin' dove?"
(She)—"I'se a flyin' lark, my Honey Love."
(He) —"Is you a bird o' one fedder, or a bird o' two?"
(She)—"I'se a bird o' one fedder w'en it comes ter you."
(He)—"Den Mam: I has desire an' quick temptation to jine my fence to yo' plantation." (Talley, p. 135.)

LULLABIES

In the division of lullabies there are two examples in Harris's collection:

1. "Nursery Song" (*Friends*, p. 213).
2. "A Howdy Song" (*Tar-Baby*, p. 187).

One of these, "Nursery Song," is sung throughout the South and is found in many varying forms. Harris's version has the following chorus:

Oh, go ter sleep! Sleepy, little babe,
  Oh, go ter sleepy, little baby,
Kaze when you wake, you'll git some cake,
  An' ride a little white horsey!

Dorothy Scarborough gives six different versions of this song.[17] There is essentially the same spirit and tune in most of the versions, but Harris's differs in that he has an initial stanza in which the situation for the song is explained:

Mammy went away—she tol' me ter stay,
An' take good keer er de baby,
She tol' me ter stay an' sing dis away;
Oh, go ter sleepy, little baby!

All the variants examined include the cakes and also ponies or "mulies" or horses. There is one stanza in the Harris version mentioning "De Booger Man" which reminds one of Dunbar's "Little Brown Baby." Other items in Harris's version which do not occur in the variants examined are silver bells, angels, a river and a boat which will rock the baby to sleep.

The theme of "A Howdy Song" is the reminiscence of an old man of the days when he coaxed the baby to get upon his knee; a recollection of the song which he sang as well as pleasant memories of the smiles and laughter of the child's response. The form is extremely intricate—there are two twelve-line stanzas for a sort of epilogue called "So long!" In the song proper the frequent repetition of *Howdy* has a drowsy effect. One stanza will serve to illustrate:

It's howdy, honey, when you sleep,
It's howdy when you cry;
Keep up, keep up de howdyin'
Don't never say good-bye!

DANCE SONG

Only one dance song is included in the ten Uncle

Remus volumes, "The Christmas Dance Song" (*Friends*, p. 197).

Alan Lomax wrote, "The Negro singer generally does not sing without dancing; even if singing in a chair his body swings and sways with the music—the arms, the hands and the feet are alive." "The Christmas Dance Song" is almost meaningless from the point of view of theme, but it furnishes the necessary rhythm. Harris wrote concerning it: "This song is sung with what Uncle Remus would call the 'knee racket'; that is to say, it is a 'patting' song. If the reader will bear in mind that the rhythmical effect is based on time—or recurring and invariable pauses—there will be no difficulty in catching the swing." [18] Use of refrain-lines may be illustrated by the first stanza:

> Rabbit foot quick, Rabbit foot light,
> —Tum-a-hash, tum-a-heap!
> Hop, skip, jump! Oh, mon, he's a sight!
> Kaze he res' all de day en run all de night,
> —Tum-a-hash, tum-a-heap,
> Oh, Rabbit-tum-a-hash!

PLAY SONGS

There are two play songs in the Remus books: "Christmas Play-Song" (S. *and* S., p. 162), and "Plantation Play-Song" (S. *and* S., p. 164). "The Christmas Play-Song" is dated 1858, Myrick Place, Putnam County. It contains folk phrases that are found in songs other than those sung by Negroes—"Hi my rinktum" and "Ho my Riley!" Christmas was one of the most delightful times on the plantations and the slaves eagerly looked forward to the dances, and other forms of merriment at that time. The high-spirited words comment on the girls, the food, and the dram.

"The Plantation Play-Song", dated Putnam County, 1856, is also a merry one. It has a refrain of eight lines, of which "Hop light, ladies, Oh, Miss Loo!" are used twice in each refrain; for example,

W'en a feller comes a knockin'
  Des holler—Oh, shoo!
Hop light, ladies,
  Oh, Miss Loo!
Oh, swing dat yaller gal!
  Do, boys, do!
Hop light, ladies,
  Oh, Miss Loo!

MISCELLANEOUS

Five songs in the Uncle Remus books must be placed under the omnibus heading, miscellaneous. They are:

1. "Run, Nigger, Run!" (*Friends*, p. 200).
2. "A Song of the Mole" (*Friends*, p. 195).
3. "A Plantation Serenade" (*S. and S.*, p. 167).
4. "De Ol' Sharp Sheep" (*Friends*, p. 207).
5. "Walk-a Chalk" (*Friends*, p. 204).

One of the most popular songs of the old plantation was "Run, Nigger, Run!" In explanation of the theme, Dorothy Scarborough wrote:

> Dr. John A. Wyeth . . . said of "Run, Nigger, Run" that it is one of the oldest of the plantation songs. White people were always afraid of an insurrection among the Negroes, and so they had a rule that no Negro should be off his plantation, especially at night, without a pass. They had patrols stationed along the roads to catch truant Negroes and the slaves called them "patter-rollers". The Negroes sang many amusing songs about the patrols and their experiences in eluding them.[19]

Some of the lines are expressive of the patrols frequently getting the wrong man; some are humorous statements of the Negro who tried to escape, who ran to the East and then to the West and finally ran his head into a hornet's nest. There are the familiar lines about that promise of "Ole Miss" which was never fulfilled:

My ole Miss, she prommus me
Dat w'en she die she set me free;
But she done dead dis many year ago,
En yer I'm a-hoein' de same ole row.

This stanza in the Harris version is similar to Talley's "Promises of Freedom" which reads:

My ole Mistiss promise me,
W'en she died, she'd set me free.
She lived so long dat 'er head got bal',
An' she give out'n de notion a dyin' at all.[20]

Talley wrote:

> There were quite a few Rhymes sung where the banjo and fiddle formed what is termed in music a simple accompaniment. Examples of these are found in "Run, Nigger, Run," and "I'll Wear Me a Cotton Dress." In such cases the music consisted of simple short tunes unquestionably "born to die." [21]

However, Harris's song has hope that a better day is coming:

But some er dese days my time will come
I'll year dat bugle, I'll year dat drum,
I'll see dem armies a-marchin' along,
I'll lif' my head en jine der song—
I'll hide no mo' behime dat tree,
W'en de angels flock fer ter wait on me!

The refrain at the end of each stanza is:

Oh, run, nigger, run! de patter-roller ketch you—
Run, nigger, run! Hit's almos' day!

"A Song of the Mole" is dated Putnam County, Georgia, 1862. There seems to be no coherent theme running throughout the selection. The habits of various birds are contrasted with those of the mole—the jay bird hunts the sparrow's nest; the bee-martin sails all around; the squirrel hollers from the top of the tree, but the mole stays in the ground.

The whipperwill hollers from across the fence—he has

no peace of mind, but the mole grabbles and digs underneath the sweet potato vine where there is no sunshine. The sparrer-hawk whets his bill on the rail, but Mr. Mole handles his two little spades down where no eye can see. The Negro works until it gets dark, and "then Mr. Mole is he"—he sings his song the whole night long where the patrols cannot see him.

The song consists of four six-line stanzas. In each stanza lines four and six are the same; one gets the idea of refrain. As is true of most of the songs in the Remus books, there is an intricate use of repetition in the refrain.

"De Ol' Sharp Sheep" is a ballad in two parts. The first episode, in stanzas one and two, tells that the old sheep was sharp when he shelled the corn by the rattle of his horn—but he wasn't so sharp when he sent it to the mill—because he sent it to the mill by the whipperwill; and the whipperwill dropped the bag and let it spill.

The other story, related in stanza three, is that Mr. Possum climbed a persimmon tree, winked his eye and grinned at a man who hit him with a rock and killed him. The man took him to the owner of the plantation; they carried him to Polly Bell who was a good cook; she made "a pie, a stew, a roast, a fry, and a barbecue."

The stanzas are of eight lines with two lines repeated twice in each stanza. There is a double interpolated refrain:

> Oh, de ole Sheep sharp w'en he shell dat corn,
> (Come along! come along!)
> He shell dat corn by de rattle er his horn,
> (Oh, do come along!)
> But he wan't so sharp when he sont it ter de mill,
> (Come along! come along!)
> Kaze he sont it ter mill by de whipperwill,
> (Oh, do come along).

There is also a refrain chorus:

De day done gone, en de night ain't long
(Do come along!)
Oh, ladies all, I mus' sing my song,
(Do come along!)

Harris indicates that "Walk-A Chalk" is found in and around Sapelo, Georgia Coast. One readily recognizes the Gullah dialect spoken by Daddy Jack in the stories. The song is composed of three five-line stanzas; each stanza ends with an exclamation:

Stanza 1: Ki! Walk-a chalk!
Stanza 2: Hi! Walk-a chalk!
Stanza 3: 'E Walk-a chalk!

Indirectly there seems to be the narration of a story of a "honkry" (hungry) man who eats rice, sops the pan, smacks his mouth, and rolls his eye. His mouth is full, he can't talk—he shuts his eye and works his jaw; he can't talk, he just "chaws and chaws"; he wipes his mouth, and shuts his eye, and stretches out as if he is going to die; he flops his head smack in the pan and dreams he hears the buckra man. It is strongly rhythmical, suggests a shuffling dance. It also suggests opportunity for pantomime.

"A Plantation Serenade" is really a song about animals, though there is nothing about the title to suggest it. Just as in the Remus stories animals play an important role, so in rhyme these creatures form one of the principal topics; he states their characteristics, talks of them as if they have the power of reason, and many of his philosophical sayings are derived from his careful observation of the "creeturs."

Talley wrote:

Many of the Folk Rhymes fall under the heading commonly denominated, "Nature Rhymes." By actual count more than a hundred and fifty recorded by the writer have something in their stanzas concerning some animal . . . It would really be more to the point to call them "Animal Rhymes" . . . Though I was brought up with the

Rhymes I make no pretensions that I really know why so many of them were made concerning the animal world.[22]

Dorothy Scarborough gives an account of a song almost identical with Harris's "A Plantation Serenade"—"Ole Bee Make De Honeycomb". A comparison of her version and Harris's may be seen in stanza two of each poem.

Harris:

De raccoon he's a cu'us man,
He never walk twel dark,
En nuthin' never 'sturbs his mine,
Twel he hear Ole Bringer bark.[23]

Scarborough:

Raccoon hunts in broad daylight,
Possum hunts in dark,
An' nuthin' never disturbs his min',
Till he hears Old Bingo bark.[24]

The first stanza in the Harris version has its counterparts in several other songs, that is, the satirical note is similar.

Harris:

De ole bee make de honey-comb,
De young bee make de honey
De niggers make de cotton en co'n
En de w'ite folks gits de money.

In Talley's Collection—"He Paid Me Seven" (Parody):

"Our Fadder, which are in Heaben!"
White man owe me leben and pay me seben.
"D'y kingdom come! D'y will be done!"
An' if I hadn't tuck dat, I wouldn' git none.[25]

Or again:

Naught's a naught, figger's a figger,
All for de white man, an' none fo' de nigger.[26]

The descriptions of the animals in three versions make an interesting comparative study.

Harris:

De raccoon totes a bushy tail,
  De 'possum totes no ha'r,
Mr. Rabbit, he come skinnin' by,
  He ain't got none ter spar'.

Scarborough:

Raccoon got de busy hair;
Opossum's tail is bare;
Rabbit ain't got no tail at all
But jes' a bunch o' hair
But jes' a bunch o' hair.[27]

Talley:

De coon's got a long ringed bushy tail,
De 'possum's tail is bare;
Dat rabbit hain't got no tail 'tall,
'Cep' a liddle bunch o' hair.[28]

Another song which has the same theme is "Squirl, He Tote a Busy Tail." [29]

SONGS INTERPOLATED IN THE STORIES

No exhaustive study has been made of the songs found in the body of the tales, but the chapter considering songs could not be concluded without at least mentioning that there are many fragments scattered throughout the Uncle Remus volumes. Frequently they are sung by some of the principal actors in the story. The largest number of these verse fragments are found in the tales in *Nights*.

Harris may have omitted songs from certain of the tales. Talley's observation in this regard is important:

> "Buckeyed Rabbit! Whoopee!" in our volume belongs with the Negro story recorded by Joel Chandler Harris under the title, "How Mr. Rabbit Lost His Fine Bushy Tail," though for some reason Mr. Harris failed to weave it into the story as was the Negro custom. "The Turtle's Song," in our collection, is another, which belongs with the story, "Mr. Terrapin Shows His Strength"; a Negro story given to the world by the same author, though the rhyme was not recorded by him.[30]

To Harris, Talley gives the credit for being among the first in literature, if not the very first, to call attention to a special feature of Negro songs and rhymes.

I now beg to offer testimony in corroboration of my assertion that Negroes had named their Rhyme parts "Call" and "Sponse." So well were these established parts of a Negro Rhyme recognized among Negroes that the whole turning point of one of their best stories was based upon it. I have reference to the Negro story recorded by Mr. Joel Chandler Harris in his "Nights with Uncle Remus," under the caption, "Brother Fox, Brother Rabbit, and King Deer's Daughter." [31]

The story to which Talley refers has this theme: Brer Fox and Brer Rabbit are both suitors of King Deer's daughter. It looks as if Brer Fox is being favored, so Brer Rabbit has to think of some ruse to subdue his opponent. Brer Rabbit kills some of King Deer's goats and tells him that Brer Fox killed them and says that Brer Fox doesn't deny it; Brer Rabbit says he will prove it in King Deer's hearing. He then enters into an agreement with Brer Fox and proposes that he [Brer Rabbit] sing the "call, lak de captain er de co'n-pile," and that Brer Fox sing the "answer" ("sponse"). "Ole Brer Rabbit, he make up de song he own se'f, en he fix it so dat he sing de call, lak de captain er de co'n-pile, en ole Brer Fox, he hatter sing de answer. . . . Ole Brer Rabbit, he got de call, en he open up lak dis:

" 'Some folks pile up mo'n dey kin tote,
En dat w'at de marter wid King Deer goat.'

en den Brer Fox, he make answer:

" 'Dat's so, dat's so, en I'm glad dat it's so!'

Den de quills en de tr'angle, dey come in, en den Brer Rabbit pursue on wid de call:

" 'Some kill sheep en some kill shote,
But Brer Fox kill King Deer goat,'

en den Brer Fox, he jine in wid de answer:

" 'I did, dat I did, en I'm glad dat I did!' "[32]

Other song fragments found in the Remus volumes, and the book in which each occurs are listed below.

1. "The Story of the Pigs" (*Nights*, p. 40). Brer Wolf sings:

> Ef you'll open de do' en let me in,
> I'll wom my han's en go home ag'in.

2. "Brother Rabbit's Riddle" (*Nights*, p. 53). Brer Rabbit sings:

> Big bird rob en little bird sing,
> De big bee zoon en little bee sting,
> De little man lead en big hoss foller—
> Kin you tell w'at's good fer a head in a holler?

Also: (*Nights*, p. 56)

> Bee-gum mighty big fer ter make Fox collar,
> Kin you tell w'at's good fer a head in a holler?

3. "How Mr. Rooster Lost His Dinner" (*Nights*, p. 60).

> Come under, come under,
> My honey, my love, my own true love;
> My heart bin a-weepin'
> Way down in Galilee.

4. "Brother Fox Covets the Quills" (*Nights*, p. 79). Brer Tarrypin sings:

> I foolee, I foolee, I foolee po' Buzzard;
> Po' Buzzard I foolee, I foolee, I foolee.

5. "A Dream and a Story" (*Nights*, p. 99). Brer Buzzud sings:

> Boo, boo, boo, my filler-mer-loo,
> Man out yer wid news fer you!

Also: (*Nights*, p. 99)

> Go 'way, go 'way, my little jug er beer,
> De news you bring, I yeard las' year.

6. "Brer Rabbit Frightens His Neighbors" (*Nights*, p. 121). Brer Rabbit sings:

> Pilly-pee, Pilly-wee!
> I see w'at he no see!
> I see, pilly-pee,
> I see w'at he no see!

7. "The Pimmerly Plum" (*Nights*, p. 225).

Good luck ter dem w'at come and go,
W'at set in de shade er de sycamo'.

Also: (*Nights*, p. 227).

Poun' er sugar, en a pint er rum,
Aint nigh so sweet ez de Pimmerly Plum!

8. "On Why Guinea-Fowls are Speckled" (*Nights*, p. 198).

Oh, Blue, go 'way! you shill not stay!
Oh, Guinny, be Gray, be Gray!

9. "Aunt Tempy's Story" (*Nights*, p. 245).

One frun sev'm
Don't leave 'lev'm.

and,

One frun six
Leaves me less kicks.

Also: (*Nights*, p. 246)

One frun five
Leaves four alive;
One frun four
Leaves th'ee un no mo';
One frun th'ee
Leaves two ter go free;
One frun one,
Un all done gone.

10. "The Fire-Test" (*Nights*, p. 249).

Lucky de Linktum, chucky de chin,
Open de do' en let me in!

Also: (*Nights*, p. 251)

I'll stay w'en you away,
'Kaze no gol' will pay toll!

11. "The Cunning Snake" (*Nights*, p. 257). The snake "talk dis sing":

Walla walla witto, me Noncy,
Walla walla witto, me Noncy,
Walla walla witto, me Noncy!

The little girl answers:

Andolee! Andoli! Andolo!

12. "The Wolf and the Horned Cattle" (*Nights*, p. 355). "Brer Rabbit holler out:

O kittle-cattle, kittle-cattle, whar yo' eyes?
Who ever see a Sook Calf snappin' at flies?"

Also

Scritchum-scratchum, lawsy, my laws!
Look at dat Sook Calf scratchin' wid claws!

Also: (*Nights*, p. 356).

Rinktum-tinktum, ride 'im on a rail!
Dat Sook Calf got a long bushy tail!

and

One un one never kin make six,
Sticks ain't hawns, un hawns ain't sticks!

13. "Mr. Hawk and Brother Buzzard" (*Nights*, p. 362). Daddy Jack sings (beating time with his foot),

T-u Tukry, t-u Ti,
T-u Tukry-Buzzud y-eye!
T-u Tukry, t-u Ting,
T-u Tukry-Buzzud wing!

14. "Brother Fox Makes a Narrow Escape" (*Nights*, p. 377). Uncle Remus sings:

O Mr. Rabbit! yo' eye mighty big—
  Yes, my Lord; dey er made fer ter see;
O Mr. Rabbit; yo' tail mighty short—
  Yes, my Lord! hit des fits me!

Also: (*Nights*, p. 380)

O Mr. Rabbit! yo' year mighty long—
  Yes, my Lord! dey made fer ter las';
O Mr. Rabbit! yo' toof mighty sharp—
  Yes, my Lord! dey cuts down grass!

15. "Fun at the Ferry" (*Friends*, p. 26). Man sings.

Oh, de rope is long, ketch a holt, ketch a holt,
  Oh, de rope is long, ketch a holt,—
A dime fer de mar', a dime fer de man,
  En a thrip fer de little gray colt.

16. "Brother Fox 'Smells Smoke'" (*Friends*, p. 60). The little boy was going through the Negro quarters yell-

ing at the top of his voice, repeating the refrain of a nonsense song he had heard the plough-hands sing.

High, my lady! Brinjer, ho.

17. "According to How the Drop Falls" (*Friends,* p. 150). Uncle Remus sings:

Virginny cut, chaw terbacker,
Nigger dance ter merlatter;
Hoe de corn, dig de tater,
Plant terbacker, 'tis no matter.

Mix de meal, fry de batter
Nigger dance ter merlatter;
Warm de cake in er platter,
Fry um in de cooney fat.

Grab er tater out de ash,
Nigger dance ter merlatter;
Possum meat dar in der platter,
Shoo! he make de nigger fatter.

18. "Why Cricket Has Elbows on His Legs" (*Told By,* p. 34). Ol Grandaddy Cricket holler back:

Hot water turn me brown,
An' den I'll kick yo' chimbley down.

19. "Brother Rabbit's Laughing Place" (*Told By,* p. 73). Uncle Remus sings:

He run ter de Eas', an he run ter de Wes'
An' jammed his head in a hornet's nest!

20. "Uncle Remus Initiates the Little Boy" (*S. and S.,* p. 21). Brer Rabbit sings:

De place wharbouts you spill de grease,
  Right dar youer boun' ter slide,
An' whar you fine a bunch er ha'r,
  You'll sholy fine de hide.

21. "Old Mr. Rabbit, He's a Good Fisherman" (*S. and S.,* p. 75). Brer Rabbit sings:

Good-by, Brer Fox, take keer yo' cloze,
Fer dis is de way de worril goes;
Some goes up en some goes down,
You'll git ter de bottom all safe en soun'.

22. "A Story about the Little Rabbits" (*S. and S.*, p. 98). A little bird sings to the little rabbits:

Take yo' toofies en gnyaw it,
Take yo' toofies en saw it,
Saw it en yoke it,
En den you kin broke it.

Also: (*S. and S.*, p. 99)

Sifter hole water same ez a tray,
Ef you fill it wid moss en dob it wid clay;
De Fox git madder de longer you stay—
Fill it wid moss en dob it with clay.

and

Spit in yo' han's en tug it en toll it,
En git behine it, en push it, en pole it;
Spit in yo' han's en r'ar back en roll it.

23. "Mr. Rabbit and Mr. Bear" (*S. and S.*, p. 100). Brer Rabbit sings:

Ti-yi! Tungalee!
I eat um pea, I pick um pea.
Hit grow in de groun', hit grow so free;
Ti-yi! dem goober pea.

24. "Mr. Bear Catches Old Mr. Bull-Frog" (*S. and S.*, p. 107). Brer Bull-frog sings:

Ingle-go-jang, my joy, my joy—
  Ingle-go-jang, my joy!
I'm right at home, my joy, my joy—
  Ingle-go-jang, my joy!

25. "The End of Mr. Bear" (*S. and S.*, p. 123). Brer Rabbit sings:

Tree stan' high, but honey might sweet—
Watch dem bees wid stingers on der feet.

26. "How Mr. Rabbit Succeeded in Raising a Dust" (*S. and S.*, p. 129). Brer Rabbit sings:

Make a bow ter de Buzzard en den ter de Crow,
Takes a limber-toe gemmun fer ter jump Jim Crow.

27. "Taily-Po" (*Returns*, p. 67). Mammy-Bammy-Big-Money sings:

Rise, skin, rise
Open yo' big red eye—
Sharpen yo' long, black claws,
An' work yo' big strong jaws!

and the wildcat sings: (*Returns*, p. 72).

Taily-po! you know an' I know
Dat I wants my Taily-po!
Over an' under an' thoo de do',
I'm a-comin' fer ter git my Taily-po!

Also: (*Returns*, p. 74)

Yo' name, I know, is Whaley-Joe
An' 'fo I'm gwineter r'a'ly go,
I'm bleeze ter have my Taily-po;
Gi' me dat an' I'll gaily go—
Taily-po! my Taily-po!

28. "How Black Snake Caught the Wolf" (*Daddy Jake*, p. 110). Mr. Black Snake sings:

Watsilla, watsilla,
Consario wo!
Watsilla, watsilla,
Consario wo!

Brer Rabbit Sings:

Watsilla, watsilla,
Bandario, wo-haw!

Also Brer Rabbit sings:

Watsilla, watsilla,
Consario wo!
Watsilla, watsilla,
Consario wo!

29. "Brother Rabbit's Courtship" (*Daddy Jake*, p. 191). One of Miss Meadows' gals sings:

Oh say de woodpecker, peckin' on de tree,
Once I courted Miss Kitty Killdee,
But she proved fickle en fum me fled,
En sence dat time my head bin red.

When she stops singing Brer Rabbit sings: (*Daddy Jake*, p. 192).

Katy, Katy! won't you marry?
  Katy, Katy! choose me den!
Mammy say ef you will marry
  She will kill de tuckey hen;
Den we'll have a new convention,
  Den we'll know de rights er men.'

30. "Daddy Jake, the Runaway" (*Daddy Jake*, pp. 37-38). Big Sam sings:

Oh, Miss Malindy, you er lots too sweet for me;
  I cannot come to see you
Ontil my time is free—
  Oh, den I'll come ter see you,
An' take you on my knee.

Oh, Miss Malindy, now don't you go away;
I cannot come to see you
Ontil some yuther day—
  Oh, den I'll come ter see you—
Oh, den I'll come ter stay.

Oh, Miss Malindy, you is my only one;
  I cannot come ter see you
Ontil de day is done—
  Oh, den I'll come ter see you,
And we'll have a little fun.

Oh, Miss Malindy, my heart belongs ter you;
  I cannot come ter see you
Ontil my work is thoo'.
  Oh, den I'll come ter see you,
I'll come in my canoe.

31. "How Black Snake Caught the Wolf" (*Daddy Jake*, p. 114). Brer Rabbit sings:

"Watsilla, watsilla,
  Consario wo!
Watsilla, watsilla,
  Consario wo!

32. "Brother Rabbit's Courtship" (*Daddy Jake*, p. 197). Brer Rabbit sings:

Some likes cake, en some likes pie,
Some loves ter laugh, en some loves ter cry,
But de gal dat stays single will die, will die!

De drouth ain't wet en de rain ain't dry,
Whar you sow yo' wheat you can't cut rye,
But de gal dat stays single will die, will die.

I wants de gal dat's atter a sign,
I wants de gal en she mus' be mine—
She'll see 'er beau down by de big pine.

33. The Field-hand's Song: "Daddy Jake, The Runaway" (*Daddy Jake*, p. 18).

My dog's a 'possum dog,
  Here, Rattler! here!
He cross de creek upon a log,
  Here, Rattler! here!

He run de 'possum up a tree,
  Here, Rattler! here!
He good enough fer you an' me,
  Here, Rattler! here!

Kaze when it comes his fat'nin time,
  Here, Rattler! here!
De 'possum eat de muscadine,
  Here, Rattler! here!

He eat till he kin skacely stan',
  Here, Rattler! here!
An' den we bake him in de pan,
  Here, Rattler! here!

34. "Mr. Crow and Brother Buzzard" (*Seven Tales*, p. 14). Mr. Crow sings:

'Susu! susu! gangook!
Muther, muther, lalho!'

and Brer Buzzard sings:

'Susu! susu! Gangook!
Muther, muther, lalho!'

In several instances, stanzas from some of the regular songs are incorporated in the stories:

1. "A Plantation Witch" (*S. and S.*, p. 136).
2. "The End of Mr. Bear" (*S. and S.*, p. 119).
3. "The Night Before Christmas" (*Nights*, p. 403).

In the songs in the Uncle Remus volumes Harris has recorded various types of folk music which subtly and characteristically express the group character of the Negro in that evanescent period of the plantation. He caught something of the spirit of the religious songs, the work songs, lullabies, dance-songs, and play-songs. He knew a great deal about the intricate use of repetition, especially in refrain. His refrains are more intricate than most folk songs. He had a definite theory of rhythm, that is, that rhythm fundamentally depends on time and not on accents. Although his fame does not rest upon the songs, they are valuable as representations of the artistic impulses so abundantly a part of Negro character in which are crystallized the thought, feeling, and universally shared lore of a folk.

AFTERWORD

If merit be aptly appraised, to Joel Chandler Harris will always go the credit for making a section famous with legends—legends which were engrafted on Southern soil. If he had done no more than give a delineation of the plantation, his place in literature would be secure. However, he did more than this—he preserved from oblivion the lore significant for an insight not only into a people but into a past.

To children, his books are perennially interesting. To those who have the capacity to use them—students of folklore, students of American literature, and lovers of literature generally—there are additional values. To all "real folks" who enjoy a good laugh and who frequently must seek an antidote to worry, the Uncle Remus books will always be a source of inestimable pleasure. Those who read but a few of the stories will find them a pleasing pastime, but those who read the ten volumes will be abundantly repaid and, I venture to predict, will find themselves going back again and again to refresh their memory, or will find themselves quoting some bit of wisdom, some quaint fragment from Harris's rich storehouse. In the Uncle Remus Books there is fancy, there is fun, there is wisdom, there is philosophy, there is literature to be relished for a lifetime.

> "Ef you hol's on ter yo' pra'rs lak you does
> ter deze yer tales yer doin' mighty well."
> —*Nights with Uncle Remus.*

APPENDIX

BRER RABBIT'S TRICKS

I. Fox

1. "Uncle Remus Initiates the Little Boy." *S. and S.*, p. 19.
2. "The Wonderful Tar-Baby Story." *S. and S.*, p. 23.
3. "How Mr. Rabbit Was Too Sharp for Mr. Fox."*S. and S.*, p. 29.
4. "Mr. Rabbit Grossly Deceives Mr. Fox" *S. and S.*, p. 34.
5. "Mr. Fox is Again Victimized." *S. and S.*, p. 39.
6. "Mr. Terrapin Appears on the Scene."*S. and S.*, p. 52.
7. "Brother Rabbit's Laughing Place." *Told By*, p. 53.
8. "Brother Fox Follows the Fashion." *Told By*, p. 53.
9. "Hello, House." *Little Boy*, p. 23.
10. "Brother Fox Smells Smoke." *Friends*, p. 60.
11. "Brother Fox Still in Trouble." *Friends*, p. 69.
12. "Brother Rabbit's Money Mint." *Friends*, p. 123.
13. "Brother Rabbit's Riddle." *Nights*, p. 51.
14. "Brother Rabbit Breaks up a Party." *Nights*, p. 61.
15. "Brother Fox, Brother Rabbit and King Deer's Daughter." *Nights*, p. 68.
16. "How Brother Fox Failed to Get His Grapes." *Nights*, p. 83.
17. "How Brother Rabbit Got the Meat." *Nights*, p. 128.
18. "Mr. Fox and Miss Goose." *Nights*, p. 3.
19. "Brother Fox Catches Mr. Horse." *Nights*, p. 8.
20. "Brother Rabbit's Astonishing Prank." *Nights*, p. 21.
21. "Aunt Tempy's Story." *Nights*, p. 241.
22. "How Brother Fox Was Too Smart." *Nights*, p. 260.
23. "Brother Rabbit Lays in His Beef Supply." *Nights*, p. 280.
24. "Brother Rabbit Rescues Brother Terrapin." *Nights*, p. 386.
25. "Brother Rabbit Gets Brother Fox's Dinner." *Nights*, p. 339.
26. "Brother Fox and the White Muscadines." *Nights*, p. 357.
27. "Brother Fox's Fish-Trap." *Nights*, p. 381.
28. "Mr. Rabbit Nibbles up the Butter." *S. and S.*, p. 75.
29. "The Moon in the Mill Pond." *Nights*, p. 100.
30. "Brother Rabbit and the Chickens." *Told By*, p. 74.

31. "Brer Rabbit and the Gold Mine." *Brer Rabbit,* p. 28.
32. "Brother Rabbit's Bear Hunt." *Returns,* p. 1.
33. "Mr. Rabbit and Mr. Bear." S. *and* S., p. 100.
34. "How Brother Rabbit Brought Family Trouble on Brother Fox." *Returns,* p. 103.
35. "Mr. Fox Gets into Serious Business." S. *and* S., p. 123.
36. "The Sad Fate of Mr. Fox." S. *and* S., p. 143.
37. "Brother Rabbit, Brother Fox and the Two Fat Pullets." *Returns,* p. 79.
38. "Old Mr. Rabbit, He's a Good Fisherman." S. *and* S., p. 72.
39. "Mr. Fox Goes A-Hunting but Mr. Rabbit Bags the Game." S. *and* S., p. 70.
40. "How the Terrapin was Taught to Fly." *Daddy Jake,* p. 123.

II. Wolf

1. "How Mr. Rabbit Saved His Meat." S. *and* S., p. 89.
2. "The Awful Fate of Mr. Wolf." S. *and* S., p. 63.
3. "Brother Wolf and the Horned Cattle." *Nights,* p. 353.
4. "Heyo, House." *Friends,* p. 142.
5. "Old Grinny Granny Wolf." *Nights,* p. 314.
6. "Brother Rabbit Pretends to be Poisoned." *Nights,* p. 297.
7. "Brother Wolf Gets in a Warm Place." *Nights,* p. 268.
8. "Brother Wolf Says Grace." *Nights,* p. 146.
9. "Cutta Cord-La." *Nights,* p. 236.
10. "Brother Rabbit Gets the Provisions." *Nights,* p. 230.
11. "Brother Wolf Falls a Victim." *Nights,* p. 208.
12. "Brother Rabbit and the Mosquitoes." *Nights,* p. 214.
13. "How Wiley Wolf Rode in the Bag." *Told By,* p. 37.
14. "How Brother Rabbit Frightened His Neighbors." *Nights,* p. 118.
15. "Mr. Wolf Makes a Failure." S. *and* S., p. 57.
16. "Brother Rabbit Takes Some Exercise." *Nights,* p. 108.
17. "Brother Rabbit's Cradle." *Told By,* p. 188.
18. "How Black Snake Caught the Wolf." *Daddy Jake,* p. 108.
19. "Mr. Goat's Short Tail." *Seven Tales,* p. 15.

III. Man

1. "Brother Rabbit and Miss Nancy." *Told By,* p. 266.
2. "Brother Rabbit Has Fun at the Ferry." *Friends,* p. 24.
3. "Mr. Man Has Some Meat." *Nights,* p. 123.

4. "In Some Lady's Garden." *Nights*, p. 177.
5. "Brother Rabbit and the Little Girl." *Nights*, p. 12.
6. "Brother Rabbit Outdoes Mr. Man." *Nights*, p. 306.

IV. All the Creeturs
1. "How Brer Rabbit Raised the Dust." *Little Boy*, p. 101.
2. "Mr. Rabbit Succeeded in Raising a Dust." *S. and S.*, p. 127.
3. "Brer Rabbit Treats the Creeturs to a Race." *Brer Rabbit*, p. 21.
4. "Brer Rabbit's Frolic." *Brer Rabbit*, p. 5.

V. Bear
1. "The End of Mr. Bear." *S. and S.*, p. 119.
2. "How Brer Rabbit Saved Brer B'ar's Life." *Little Boy*, p. 69.
3. "Brother Bear and the Honey Orchard." *Friends*, p. 12.
4. "Brother Bear Learns to Comb His Head." *Seven Tales*, p. 23.

VI. Lion
1. "Brother Rabbit Ties Mr. Lion." *Nights*, p. 325.
2. "Brother Rabbit Conquers Brother Lion." *Friends*, p. 134.

VII. Hawk
1. "Mr. Hawk and Brother Rabbit." *Nights*, p. 366.

VIII. Buzzard
1. "Brer Rabbit's Flying Trip." *Brer Rabbit*, p. 22.

IX. Cow
1. "Miss Cow Falls a Victim to Mr. Rabbit." *S. and S.*, p. 47.

X. Alligator
1. "Brother Rabbit and the Gizzard Eater." *Told By*, p. 243.

XI. Tiger
1. "Brother Rabbit Frightens Brother Tiger." *Friends*, p. 101.

XII. Wildcat
1. "Brother Rabbit and Mr. Wildcat." *Nights*, p. 286.

XIII. Opossum
1. "Brother 'Possum Gets in Trouble." *Nights*, p. 185.

XIV. Weasel
1. "How Wattle Weasel Was Caught." *Nights*, p. 319.

XV. Dog
1. 'Why Mr. Dog Runs Brother Rabbit." *Nights*, p. 349.

FOLK-LORE OF THE SOUTHERN NEGROES

By WILLIAM OWENS *

All tribes and peoples have their folk-lore, whether embodied in tales of daring adventure, as in our own doughty Jack, the Giant-killer, or in stories of genii and magic, as in the *Arabian Nights*, or in legends of wraiths, witches, bogles, and apparitions, as among the Scotch peasantry; and these fables are so strongly tinged with peculiarities—or rather the idiosyncrasies—of the race among whom they originate as to furnish a fair index of its mental and moral characteristics, not only at the time of their origin, but so long as the people continue to narrate them or listen to them.

The folk-lore of Africo-Americans, as appearing in our Southern States, is a medley of fables, songs, sayings, incantations, charms and superstitious traditions brought from various tribes along the West African coast, and so far condensed into one mass in their American homes that often part of a story or tradition belonging to one tribe is grafted, without much regard to consistency, upon a part belonging to another people, while they are still further complicated by the frequent infusion into them of ideas evidently derived from communication with the white race.

Any one who will take the trouble to analyze the predominant traits of negro character, and to collate them with the predominant traits of African folk-lore, will discern the fitness of each to each. On every side he will discover the evidences of a passion for music and dancing, for visiting and chatting, for fishing and snaring, indeed for any pleasure requiring little exertion of either mind or body; evidences also of a gentle, pliable and easy temper—of a quick and sincere sympathy with suffering wheresoever seen—of a very low standard of morals, combined with remarkable dexterity in satisfying themselves that it is right to do as they wish. Another trait, strong enough and universal enough to atone for many a dark one, is that, as a rule, there is nothing of the fierce and cruel in their nature, and it is scarcely possible for anything of this kind to be grafted permanently upon them.

Of their American-born superstitions, by far the greater part are interwoven with so-called religious beliefs, and go far to show their

* Published in *Lippincott's Magazine*, December, 1877.

native faith in dreams and visions, which they are not slow to narrate, to embellish, and even to fabricate extemporaneously, to suit the ears of a credulous listener; also showing their natural tendency to rely upon outward observances, as if possessed of some *fetish*-like virtue, and in certain cases a horrible debasement of some of the highest and noblest doctrines of the Christian faith. These superstitions must of course be considered apart from the real character of those who are sincerely pious, and upon which they are so many blemishes. They are, in fact, the rank and morbid outgrowth of the peculiarities of religious denominations grafted upon the prolific soil of their native character.

Of the few which may be mentioned without fear of offence, since they belong to the negro rather than to his denomination, the following are examples: Tools to be used in digging a grave must never be carried through a house which any one inhabits, else they will soon be used for digging the grave of the dweller. Tools already used for such a purpose must not be carried directly home. This would bring the family too closely for safety into contact with the dead. They must be laid reverently beside the grave, and allowed to remain there all night. A superstition in respect to posture is by some very rigorously observed. It is that religious people must never sit with their legs crossed. The only reason given—though we cannot help suspecting that there must be another kept in concealment—is, that *crossing the legs is the same as dancing, and dancing is a sin.*

These are fair samples of Americanized superstitions—puerile, it is true, but harmless. It is only when we come into contact with negroes of pure African descent that we discover evidences of a once prevalent and not wholly discarded demonolatry. The native religion of the West African, except where elevated by the influence of Mohammedanism, was not—and, travellers tell us, is not yet—a worship of God as such, nor even an attempt to know and honor Him, but a constant effort at self-protection. The true God, they say, calls for no worship; for, being good in and of himself, He will do all the good He can without being asked. But there are multitudes of malignant spirits whose delight is to mislead and to destroy. These must be propitiated by gifts and acts of worship, or rendered powerless by charms and incantations.

No one knows, or has the means of ascertaining, to what extent real devil-worship is practised in America, because it is always conducted in secret; but we have reason to believe that it has almost entirely ceased, being shamed out of existence by the loveliness of a purer and better faith, and a belief in the agency of evil spirits, and consequent dread of their malign powers, although still more or less dominant with the negroes, has already greatly declined.* To give a sample of this last: The time was—but it has nearly passed away, or else the writer has not been for many years in the way of hearing of it, as in the days of childhood—when one of the objects of greatest dread among our seaboard negroes was the "Jack-muh-lantern." This terrible creature—who on dark, damp nights would wander with his lantern through woods and marshes, seeking to mislead people to their destruction—was described by a negro who seemed perfectly familiar with his subject as a hideous little being, somewhat human in form, though covered with hair like a dog. It had great goggle eyes, and thick, sausage-like lips that opened from ear to ear. In height, it seldom exceeded four or five feet, and it was quite slender in form, but such was its power of locomotion that no one on the swiftest horse could overtake it or escape from it, for it could leap like a grasshopper to almost any distance, and its strength was beyond all human resistance. No one ever heard of its victims being bitten or torn: they were only compelled to go with it into the bogs and swamps and marshes, and there left to sink and die. There was only one mode of escape for those who were so unfortunate as to be met by one of these mischievous nightwalkers, and that was by a charm; but that charm was easy and within everybody's reach. Whether met by marsh or roadside, the person had only to take off his coat or outer garment and put it on again inside out, and the foul fiend was instantly deprived of all power to harm.

Multifarious, however, as are the forms and aspects of folk-lore among this remarkable and in some respects highly interesting people, the chief bulk of it lies stored away among their fables, which are as purely African as are their faces or their own plaintive melodies. Travellers and missionaries tell us that the same sweet airs which are so often heard in religious meetings in America, set to Christian hymns,

* Of the terrible forms of superstition prevalent under the names of Obi, Voodooism, Evil-eye or Tricking, in which a trick-doctor or witch-doctor works against another person's life or health or plans, or seeks to neutralize the influence of another doctor, our subject leads us to say nothing.

are to be recognized in the boats and palm-roofed houses of Africa, set to heathen words, and that the same wild stories of Buh Rabbit, Buh Wolf, and other *Buhs* that are so charming to the ears of American children, are to be heard to this day in Africa, differing only in the drapery necessary to the change of scene.

Almost without exception the actors in these fables are brute animals endowed with speech and reason, in whom mingle strangely, and with ludicrous incongruity, the human and brute characteristics. The *dramatis personae* are always honored with the title of *Buh,* which is generally supposed to be an abbreviation of the word "brother" (the *br* being sounded without the whir of the *r*), but it probably is a title of respect equivalent to our Mr. The animals which figure in the stories are chiefly Buh Rabbit, Buh Lion, Buh Wolf and Buh Deer, though sometimes we hear of Buh Elephant, Buh Fox, Buh Cooter and Buh Goose. As a rule, each Buh sustains in every fable the same general character. Buh Deer is always a simpleton; Buh Wolf always rapacious and tricky; Buh Rabbit foppish, vain, quick-witted, though at times a great fool; Buh Elephant quiet, sensible and dignified.

Of the Buh fables, that which is by all odds the greatest favorite, and which appears in the greatest variety of forms, is the "Story of Buh Rabbit and the Tar Baby." Each variation preserves the great landmarks, particularly the closing scene. According to the most thoroughly African version, it runs thus: Buh Rabbit and Buh Wolf are neighbors. In a conversation one day Buh Wolf proposes that they two shall dig a well for their joint benefit, instead of depending upon chance rainfalls or going to distant pools or branches, as they often have to do, to quench their thirst. To this Buh Rabbit, who has no fondness for labor, though willing enough to enjoy its fruits, offers various objections, and finally gives a flat refusal.

"Well," says Buh Wolf, who perfectly understands his neighbor, "if you no help to dig well, you musn't use de water."

"What for I gwine use de water?" responds Buh Rabbit with affected disdain. "What use I got for well? In de mornin' I drink de dew, an' in middle o' day I drink from de cow-tracks."

The well is dug by Buh Wolf alone, who after a while perceives that some one besides himself draws from it. He watches, and soon identifies the intruder as Buh Rabbit, who makes his visits by night. "Ebery mornin' he see Buh Rabbit tracks—ebery mornin' Buh Rabbit tracks." Indignant at the intrusion, he resolves to set a trap for his thievish neighbor and to put him to death. Knowing Buh Rabbit's buckish love for the ladies, he fits up a *tar baby* made to look like a beautiful girl, and sets it near the well. By what magical process this manufacture of an attractive-looking young lady out of treacherous adhesive tar is accomplished we are not informed. But listeners to stories must not be inquisitive about the mysterious parts; they must be content to hear.

Buh Rabbit, emboldened by long impunity, goes to the well as usual after dark, sees this beautiful creature standing there motionless, peeps at it time and time again suspiciously; but being satisfied that it is really a young lady, he makes a polite bow and addresses her in gallant language. The young lady makes no reply. This encourages him to ask if he may not come to take a kiss. Still no reply. He sets his water-bucket on the ground, marches up boldly and obtains the kiss, but finds to his surprise that he cannot get away; his lips are held fast by the tar. He struggles and tries to persuade her to let him go. How he is able to speak with his lips sticking fast is another unexplained mystery; but no matter: he does speak, and most eloquently, yet in vain. He now changes his tone, and threatens her with a slap. Still no answer. He administers the slap, and his hand sticks fast. One after the other, both hands and both feet, as well as his mouth, are thus caught, and poor Buh Rabbit remains a prisoner until Buh Wolf comes the next morning to draw water.

"Eh! eh! Buh Rabbit, wah de matter?" exclaims Buh Wolf, affecting the greatest surprise at his neighbor's woeful plight.

Buh Rabbit, who has as little regard for truth as for honesty, replies, attempting to throw all the blame upon the deceitful maiden by whom he has been entrapped, not even suspecting yet—so we are to infer—that she is made of tar instead of living flesh. He declares with all the earnestness of injured innocence that he was passing by, in the sweet, honest moonlight, in pursuit of his lawful business, when this girl *hailed* him, and decoyed him into giving her a kiss, and was now holding him in unlawful durance.

The listener ironically commiserates his captive neighbor, and proposes to set him free; when, suddenly noticing the water-bucket and the tracks by the well, he charges Buh Rabbit with his repeated robberies by night, and concludes by declaring his intention to put him to immediate death.

The case has now become pretty serious, and Buh Rabbit is of course woefully troubled at the near approach of the great catastrophe; still, even in this dire extremity, his wits do not cease to cheer him with some hope of escape. Seeing that his captor is preparing to hang him—for the cord is already around his neck and he is being dragged toward an overhanging limb—he expresses the greatest joy by capering, dancing and clapping his hands—so much so that the other curiously inquires, "What for you so glad, Buh Rabbit?"

"Oh," replies the sly hypocrite, "because you gwine hang me and not trow me in de brier-bush."

"What for I mustn't trow you in de brier-bush?" inquires Mr. Simpleton Wolf.

"Oh," prays Buh Rabbit with a doleful whimper, "please hang me; please trow me in de water or trow me in de fire, where I die at once. But don't—oh don't trow me in de brier-bush to tear my poor flesh from off my bones."

"I gwine to do 'zactly wah you ax me not to do," returns Wolf in savage tones. Then, going to a neighboring patch of thick, strong briers, he pitches Buh Rabbit headlong in the midst, and says, "now let's see de flesh come off de bones."

No sooner, however, does the struggling and protesting Buh Rabbit find himself among the briers than he slides gently to the ground, and peeping at his would-be torturer from a safe place behind the stems, he says, "Tankee, Buh Wolf—a thousand tankee—for *bring me home!* De brier-bush *de berry place where I been born.*"

Another favorite story is that of the "Foot-Race." Buh Rabbit and Buh Frog are admirers of the beautiful Miss Dinah, and try their best to win her. The lady likes them both, but not being permitted to marry both, she resolves to make her choice depend upon the result of a foot-race. The distance is to be ten miles—that is, five miles out and five miles in—along a level road densely bordered with bushes. The day arrives. Miss Dinah, seated at the starting-point, is to give the word to the rivals, who stand one on either side, and the goal for the winner is to be a place *in her lap.* By agreement, Buh Rabbit is to take the open road, and Buh Frog, who prefers it, is allowed to leap through the bushes, and both are to hallo to each other at the end of every mile. Buh Rabbit, however, with all his cunning, has this time met his match; for Buh Frog has engaged five of his kinsmen, so nearly like himself in appearance that they cannot be distinguished from him, and has stationed one in concealment near each mile-post, with instructions how to act, while he has provided for himself a nice hiding-place in the bushes near Miss Dinah's seat. At the word Go! the rivals start, Buh Frog leaping into the bushes, where he disappears, and Buh Rabbit capering along the road and flaunting his white tail merrily at the thought of distancing the other so far that he shall never see or hear of him again till after Miss Dinah has been won. At the end of the first mile Buh Rabbit turns his head back and tauntingly halloos, "I here, Buh Frog! How you git 'long?"

To his dismay, however, he hears the voice of the other in the bushes ahead of him singing out, "Boo-noo! I here too! I beat you here, I'll beat you there; I'll beat you back to Miss Dinah's lap!"

On hearing this boast repeated ahead of him in the bushes at each mile-post, Buh Rabbit becomes frantic, and rushes through the last mile as he had never run before. But all in vain. Just as he comes within easy view of the coveted goal he sees Buh Frog leap from the bushes plump into Miss Dinah's lap, and hears him sing, with as good breath as though he had not run a mile,

"Boo-noo! Before you!
I beat you there, I beat you here:
I've beat you back to Miss Dinah's lap!"

Another version makes the competitors Buh Deer and Buh Cooter (the negro name for terrapin or land-tortoise), in which Buh Cooter wins the day by collusion with some of his closely-resembling kin. Substantially the same story is to be heard from the natives of each of the four continents, but whether the African gained his idea of it from Europe or Asia, or whether the European or Asian gained it from Africa, is perhaps past determining. The writer can testify that the story as above narrated, or rather the substance of it, was told him in childhood by negroes supposed to have obtained it direct from Africa.

Some of these stories are mere laudations of Buh Rabbit's shrewdness and common sense. Buh Wolf has long had a watering of the mouth for rabbit-flesh, but has never been able to gratify it. He finally hits upon the following expedient: He causes a report to be spread that he has suddenly died, and all his neighbors, especially Buh Rabbit, are invited to his funeral. He has no doubt that his plump, short-tailed neighbor, being once enclosed within the walls of his house, will fall an easy prey to himself and his attending cousins. Buh Rabbit, however, is not to be easily ensnared. He goes demurely to the house of mourning, but does not enter. He seats himself on the steps by the side of Buh Cat, who is enjoying the sunshine in the doorway.

"Is Buh Wolf dead, for true and true?" he inquires.

"I suppose so. Eberybody say he dead," answers Buh Cat.

"How did he die, and when?" he continues to inquire.

Buh Cat gives the particulars as reported to him, and Buh Rabbit pretends to receive them with all faith, expressing great sorrow for the loss experienced by the neighborhood. But after a little musing he seems to be struck with a new idea, and turning to Buh Cat he inquires in hopeful tone, "But did he *grin or whistle* before he died? People who die *must* do one or t'other; and some, who die hard, do both. I'm a doctor, you know."

This is said in the doorway, near the stiff-looking corpse, and in a whisper loud enough to be heard all through the room. Very soon Buh Wolf is heard to whistle, and then his lips settle into a grin so broad as to show his teeth.

"Buh Cat," says Buh Rabbit, putting his hand on his stomach and screwing up his face as if seized with mortal sickness, "I mus' hurry home and take some yarb tea, or mebbe I'll have to grin and whistle like our poor neighbor. Goodbye, Buh Cat. Come to me, please, after Buh Wolf done berry and tell me all about it. Good-bye."

To the surprise of all who are not in the secret, the corpse gives a loud sneeze, then leaps from the table, throws off his "berryin' clothes," and joins his friends in eating heartily of his own funeral dinner.

His hankering, however, for rabbit-mutton still continues, and he resolves, notwithstanding his recent inglorious defeat, to attempt again to gratify it. With this end in view he makes frequent visits to his neighbor and talks with him across the fence, but is never invited beyond. One day, in the course of conversation, he informs him that there is a fine pear tree on the other side of a neighboring field, loaded with luscious fruit just in condition to be gathered.

"I will go get some."

"When?"

"To-morrow, when the sun is about halfway up the sky."

"Go: I will join you there."

Buh Rabbit rises very early, goes to the tree soon after daybreak, finds the pears uncommonly good, and is laughing to himself to think how he has outwitted his enemy, when he hears a voice under the tree: "Ho, Mr. Rabbit! in the tree a'ready?"

"Yes," replies Buh Rabbit, trembling at the sight of his dreaded foe: "I wait for you, and tink you nebber gwine come. I tell you w'at," smacking his lips, "dem here pear too good."

"Can't you trow me down some?" inquires Buh Wolf, so strongly impressed by the sound of that eloquent smack that he longs to get a taste of the fruit.

Buh Rabbit selects some of the finest, which he throws far off in the soft grass, in order, he says to avoid bruising, and while Buh Wolf is engaged in eating them, with his head buried in the grass, Buh Rabbit slides quietly from the tree and hurries home.

A few days thereafter Buh Wolf makes still another attempt. He pays a visit as before, and speaks of a great fair to be held next day in a neighboring town. "I am going," says the rash Buh Rabbit; and he does go, although we might suppose that he would have sense enough to keep out of harm's way. On returning home, late in the day, he sees Buh Wolf sitting on a log by the roadside, at the bottom of a hill, waiting for him. His preparations for escape have already been made in the purchase of a quantity of hollow tinware. Slipping quietly into the bushes, without being seen by the way-layer, he puts a big tin mug on his head and a tin cup on each hand and foot, and, hanging various tin articles around his body, he comes rolling down down the hill toward Buh Wolf, who is so frightened at the unearthly noise that he runs off with his tail between his legs, and never troubles Buh Rabbit again.

The struggle between them, however, does not cease even with this trumph of the weaker party. There is a contest now of love and strategem. They both pay their addresses to the same young lady, making their visits to her on alternate evenings. In the progress of the courtship Buh Rabbit learns that his rival has spoken of him contemptuously, saying that he is very dressy and foppish, it is true, but that he has no manliness; adding that he (Buh Wolf) could eat him up at a mouthful. To this Buh Rabbit retorts the next evening by assuring Miss Dinah that Buh Wolf was nothing but his grandfather's old *riding horse;* adding "I ride him, and whip him too, whenever I choose, and he obeys me like a dog." The next afternoon Buh Rabbit tempts his unsuspecting rival to join him in the play of riding horse, which consists in each in turn mounting the other's back and riding for a while. Buh Rabbit, who has thought out the whole case beforehand offers to give the first ride, and so times it that the ride ends at his own door about the time for the usual visit to Miss Dinah. He runs into the house and puts on his dandy clothes, pleading that he cannot enjoy a ride unless he is in full dress; and pleading, moreover, that he cannot ride without saddle and bridle and all that belongs to a horseman, he persuades Mr. Fool Wolf to allow a strong, rough bit to be put into his mouth and a close-fitting saddle to be girded to his back, upon which Buh Rabbit mounts, holding in his hand a terrible whip and having his heels armed with a pair of long sharp spurs. Thus accoutred, he prevails upon Buh Wolf to take the road toward Miss Dinah's house, on approaching which he so vigorously applies both whip and spur as to compel his resisting steed to trot up to the door, where Buh Rabbit bows politely to his lady-love, saying, "I told you so; now you see for yourself." Of course he wins the bride.

There is a class of stories approaching somewhat in character those related of our own Jack the Giant-killer, leaving out the giants. The one given below seems to have a common origin with the Anglo-Saxon story of the "Three Blue Pigs." This is entitled "Tiny Pig."

A family of seven pigs leave home to seek their fortunes, and settle in a neighborhood harassed by a mischievous fox. Each of these pigs builds himself a house of dirt, except Tiny Pig, who, though the runt of the litter, is a sensible little fellow and the hero of the tale. He builds his house of stone, with good strong doors and a substantial chimney. In due course of time, Fox, being hungry, comes to the house of one of the brothers, and asks to be admitted, but is refused. The request and refusal, as told by the negroes, is couched in language which is intended to be poetical, and is certainly not without some pretension to the picturesque. Fox's request in each case is—

"Mr. Pig, Mr. Pig, oh let me in;
I'll go away soon, and not touch a thing."

and the refusal is—

"No, no, Mr. Fox, by the beard on my chin!
You may say what you will, but I'll not let you in."

On being refused, Fox threatens to *blow down* the house and eat up the occupant. Pig continuing to refuse—as what pig would not?—the house is blown down and the owner eaten up. This sad fate befalls in turn each of the six who had been so foolish or so lazy as to build their houses of dirt. Fox, having finished all six, and becoming again hungry, comes at last to the stone house, where he makes the same hypocritical request, and meets the same heroic refusal. He now threatens to blow down the house. "Blow away and welcome!" retorts the little hero. Fox blows "until his wind gives out," but cannot move the first stone. He then tries scratching and tearing with his paws, but only succeeds in tearing off two of his own toe-nails. "I will come down your chimney," he threatens, leaping as he says so to the roof of the house. "Come soon as you please," sturdily replies Tiny Pig, standing before his fireplace with a big armful of dry straw ready to be thrown upon the fire. As soon as Fox has entered the chimney, and come down too far to return quickly, Tiny Pig throws the dry straw upon the fire, which creates such a blaze that Fox is scorched and smoked to death, and Tiny Pig lives the rest of his life in peace, the hero of his neighborhood.

This story certainly furnishes foundation for a moral which we will leave the reader to construct for himself, remarking as we pass that, so far as we know, no moral has ever been drawn. Several other stories may be regarded as inculcating, though feebly, some moral precept.

One of these bears some features of American negro life, grafted probably upon African stock: The denizens of a certain farmyard—ducks, geese, turkeys, pea-fowls, guinea-fowls, hens, roosters and all—were invited by those of another farmyard to a supper and a dance. They all went as a matter of course, headed by the big farmyard rooster, who strutted and crowed as he marched. They were a merry set, and such an amount of quacking, cackling and gabbling as they made was seldom heard. After a few rounds of dancing, just to give them a better appetite for supper and fit them for a longer dance afterward, they were introduced to the supper-room. There they saw on the table a pyramid of eatables high as the old gobbler's head when stretched to its utmost; but, alas! it was, or seemed to be, a pyramid of *corn bread* only—pones upon pones of it, yet nothing but corn bread.

On seeing this the rooster becomes very indignant, and struts out of the house, declaring that he will have nothing to do with so mean a supper, for he can get corn bread enough at home. As he is angrily going off, however, the others, who are too hungry to disdain even the plainest fare, fall to work; and no sooner has the outer layer of corn loaves been removed—for it is only the outer layer—than they find within a huge pile of bacon and greens, and at the bottom of the pile, covered and protected by large dishes, any amount of pies and tarts and cakes and other good things.

Poor Rooster looks wistfully back, and is sorry that he had made that rash speech. But it is too late now, for his word is out, and no one ever knew Rooster to take back his word if he had to die for it. He learned, however, a valuable lesson that night, for from that time to this it has been observed that Rooster always *scratches* with his feet the place where he finds, or expects to find, anything to eat, and that he never leaves off scratching until he has searched to the bottom.

Our last story is more purely African, at least in its *dramatis personae*. Buh Elephant and Buh Lion were one day chatting upon various subjects, when the elephant took occasion to say that he was afraid of no being on earth except man. On seeing the big boastful eyes of the lion stretching wider and his mane bristling, as if in disdain, he added, "you know, Buh Lion, that, although you are held as the most to be dreaded of all beasts, I am not afraid of any of your tribe, for if any of them should attack me I could receive him on my tusk, or strike him dead with my trunk, or even shake him off from my body and then trample him to death under my feet. But man—who can kill us from a distance with his guns and arrows, who can set traps for us of which we have no suspicion, who can fight us from the backs of horses so swift that we can neither overtake him nor escape from him—I do fear, for neither strength, nor courage, can avail against his wisdom."

Buh Lion, on hearing this, shook himself, and said that he was no more afraid of man than he was of any other creature which he was in the habit of eating; and added that the only beings on earth he was afraid of were *partridges*.

"Partridges!" exclaims Buh Elephant in wonder. "What do you mean?"

"Why this," says Buh Lion, "That when I am walking softly through the woods I sometimes rouse a covey of partridges, and then they rise all around me with such a whir as to make me start. I am afraid of nothing but partridges."

Not long afterward Buh Elephant heard a gun fired near a neighboring village, followed by a loud, prolonged roar. Going there to learn what was the matter, he saw Buh Lion lying dead by the roadside with a great hole in his body made by a musketball. "Ah, my poor friend," he said, "partridges could never have treated you in this way."

BIBLIOGRAPHY

BOOKS BY HARRIS

Aaron in the Wildwoods. Illustrated by Oliver Herford. Boston: Houghton, Mifflin & Co., 1897.

Reviews. "Dial," 23:344; "Academy," 52:480; "Literary World," 29:62; "Athenaeum," 2:252.

Balaam and his Master, and Other Sketches and Stories. Boston: Houghton, Mifflin & Co., 1891.

The Bishop and the Boogerman. Illustrated by Charlotte Harding. New York: Doubleday, Page & Co., 1909.

Chronicles of Aunt Minerva Ann. Illustrated by A. B. Frost. New York: Charles Scribner's Sons, 1899.

Review. "Bookbuyer," 19:290.

Daddy Jake the Runaway, and Short Stories told after Dark. Illustrated by E. W. Kemble. New York: Century Company, 1889.

Free Joe, and Other Georgian Sketches. New York: Charles Scribner's Sons, 1887.

Gabriel Tolliver, a Story of Reconstruction. New York. McClure, Phillips & Co., 1902.

Reviews. "Dial," 34:243; "Nation," 75:467; "Bookbuyer," 25:623; "Critic," n.s., 41:581.

Little Mr. Thimblefinger and his Queer Country; What the Children Saw and Heard There. Illustrated by Oliver Herford. Boston: Houghton, Mifflin & Co., 1894.

For sequel see "Mr. Rabbit at Home."

Little Union Scout. Illustrated by George Gibbs: a Tale of Tennessee during the Civil War. New York: McClure, Phillips & Co., 1904.

Making of a Statesman, and Other Stories. New York: McClure, Phillips & Co., 1902.

Reviews. "Dial," 32:389; "Nation," 74:471.

Mingo, and Other Sketches in Black and White. Boston: James R. Osgood & Co., 1884.

Review. "Nation, 39:115.

Mr. Rabbit at Home (a sequel to Little Mr. Thimblefinger). Illustrated by Oliver Herford. Boston: Houghton, Mifflin & Co., 1895.

Nights with Uncle Remus: Myths and Legends of the Old Plantation. Illustrated by F. S. Church. Boston: James R. Osgood & Co., 1883.

Review. "Nation," 37:422.

On the Plantation; A Story of a Georgia Boy's Adventures during the War. Illustrated by E. W. Kemble. New York: D. Appleton & Co., 1892.

Autobiographical.

Review. "Dial," 13.46.

On the Wing of Occasions; Being the Authorized Version of Certain Curious Episodes of the Late Civil War, Including the Hitherto Suppressed Narrative of the Kidnapping of President Lincoln. New York: Doubleday, Page & Co., 1900.

Also published under the title of "The Kidnapping of President Lincoln."

Plantation Pageants. Illustrated by E. Boyd Smith. Boston: Houghton, Mifflin & Co., 1899.

Seven Tales of Uncle Remus. Edited by Thomas H. English. Emory University. Sources and Reprints, 1948.

Shadow Between His Shoulder Blades. Boston: Small, Maynard & Co., 1909.

Sister Jane, Her Friends and Acquaintances; A Narrative of Certain Events and Episodes Transcribed from the Papers of the Late William Wornum. Boston: Houghton, Mifflin & Co., 1896.

Stories of Georgia. Illustrated by A. I. Keller, Guy Rose, B. W. Clinedinst, and others. New York: American Book Co., 1896.

Story of Aaron (so named), the Son of Ben Ali, Told by his Friends and Acquaintances. Illustrated by Oliver Herford. Boston: Houghton, Mifflin & Co., 1896.

Tales of the Home Folks in Peace and War. Boston: Houghton, Mifflin & Co., 1898.

Reviews. "Public Opinion," 24:537; "Outlook," 58:1078; "Nation," 66:407; "Bookman," 7:353; "Independent," 50:729; "Bookbuyer," 17:62; "Critic," n.s., 30:204.

Tar-Baby, and Other Rhymes of Uncle Remus. Illustrated by A. B. Frost and E. W. Kemble. New York: D. Appleton & Co., 1904.

Told by Uncle Remus; New Stories of the Old Plantation. Illustrated by A. B. Frost, J. M. Frost, J. M. Conde, and Frank Verbeck. New York: McClure, Phillips & Co., 1905.

Reviews. "Critic," 47:576; "Independent," 59:1385; "Dial," 39:444; "Nation," 81:407; "New York Times," 10:864; "Review of Reviews," 32:753.

Uncle Remus and Brer Rabbit. New York: Frederick A. Stokes, 1906.

Uncle Remus and his Friends: Old Plantation Stories, Songs and Ballads, with Sketches of Negro Character. Illustrated by A. B. Frost. Boston: Houghton, Mifflin & Co., 1892.

Uncle Remus and the Little Boy. Boston: Small, Maynard & Co., 1910.
A collection of stories and rhymes appearing in "Uncle Remus's Magazine" during 1907 and 1908.

Uncle Remus, His Songs and His Sayings. Illustrated by F. S. Church and J. H. Moser. New York: D. Appleton & Co., 1880. Edition of 1906 illustrated by A. B. Frost.
Reviews. "Nation," 31:398; "Spectator," 445; "Current Literature," 29:708.

Uncle Remus Returns. Boston: Houghton, Mifflin Co., 1918.
A collection of stories and sketches appearing in the *Metropolitan Magazine,* 1905 and 1906, and *The Atlanta Constitution.*

Wally Wanderoon and his Story-Telling Machine. Illustrated by Karl Moseley. New York: McClure, Phillips & Co., 1903.

TRANSLATION BY HARRIS

Evening Tales. Translated from the French of Frederic Ortoli. New York: Charles Scribner's Sons, 1893.

INTRODUCTIONS BY HARRIS

Field, Eugene. *Complete Works.* New York: Charles Scribner's Sons.

Frost, A. B. *Drawings, with verses by Wallace Irwin.* New York: Richard K. Fox, 1905.

Goulding, F. R. *Young Marooners.* New York: Dodd, Mead & Co.

Knight, L. L. *Reminiscences of Famous Georgians.* Atlanta: Franklin Co., 1907.

Russell, Irwin. *Poems.* New York: Century Co.

Stanton, F. L. *Songs of a Day.* Atlanta: Foote & Davies, 1893.

Stanton, F. L. *Songs of The Soil.* New York: D. Appleton & Co., 1894.

Weeden, Howard. *Bandanna Ballads.* New York: Doubleday, Page & Co., 1899.

EDITED BY HARRIS

Library of Southern Literature. Edwin Anderson Alderman, Joel Chandler Harris, editors in chief; Charles William Kent, literary editor. New Orleans, Atlanta, etc.: Martin & Hoyt Company, 1908-1913.

Life of Henry W. Grady. New York: Cassell, 1890.
Merrymaker. Boston: Hall, Locke & Company, 1902. Issued in 1901 under the title *The Book of Fun and Frolic.*
World's Wit and Humor. New York: Doubleday, Page & Co., 1904.

BOOKS IN WHICH APPEAR SKETCHES OF HARRIS

Avary, Mrs. Myrta (Lockett). *Joel Chandler Harris and His Home: A Sketch.* Atlanta, Ga.: Appeal Publishing Co. 1913. 38 pages. Authorized by the Uncle Remus Memorial Association. Eleven portraits of Mr. Harris, showing him from boyhood. Thirty illustrations. The most extensive of the various sketches.

Bardeen, Charles William. *Authors' Birthdays.* Second series. Syracuse, N. Y.: C. W. Bardeen. 1899. 459 pages. Standard Teachers' Library. *Joel Chandler Harris,* pages 427-459.

Baskervill, William Malone. *Life of Uncle Remus.* Nashville, Tenn.: Barbee Publishing Company.

Baskervill, William Malone. *Southern Writers: Biographical and Critical Studies.* Volume I. Nashville, Tenn.: Publishing House M. E. Church, South. 1897. 404 pages. "Joel Chandler Harris," pages 41-88. First issued in pamphlet form, July, 1896, by same Publishing House.

Bradley, Henry Stiles. *Library of Southern Literature.* New Orleans, Atlanta, etc.: Martin & Hoyt Co. 1908-1913. "Joel Chandler Harris." Volume V., pages 2111-2151.

Brainerd, Erastus. *Joel Chandler Harris at Home.* (See Gilder, J. L. *Authors at Home.* Pages 111-124. Wessels. 1902.) Same article appeared in the *Critic,* May 16, 23, 1885, Volume VI, pages 229-241.

Davidson, James Wood. *The Living Writers of the South.* New York: Carleton. 1869.

Derby, James Cephas. *Fifty Years among Authors, Books, and Publishers.* New York: G. W. Carleton & Co. 1884.

Fiske, Horace Spencer. *Provincial Types in American Fiction.* Chautauqua, N. Y.: Chautauqua Press. 1903. 264 pages. Chautauqua Home Reading Series. "Joel Chandler Harris," pages 106-117.

Halsey, Francis Whiting, editor. *Authors of Our Day in Their Homes.* New York: Pott. 1902.

Harkins, Edward Francis. *Little Pilgrimages among the Men Who Have Written Famous Books.* Boston: L. C. Page & Co. 1902.

Holliday, Carl. *History of Southern Literature.* New York: Neale. 1906.

Kellner, Leon. *Geschichle der Nordamerikanischen Literatur.* Berlin and Leipsig. 1913. Gives the Tar Baby story in German. Translated by Julia Franklin and published by Doubleday in 1915.

Knight, Lucian Lamar. *Reminiscences of Famous Georgians.* Atlanta, Ga.: Franklin-Turner Co. 1907-08. Two volumes. "Joel Chandler Harris," Volume I., pages 482-492.

Lee, Ivy Ledbetter, compiler. *Uncle Remus.* Joel Chandler Harris as seen and remembered by a few of his friends, including a memorial sermon by the Rev. James W. Lee, D.D., and a poem by Frank L. Stanton. Privately printed. 1908.

Library of the World's Best Literature. C. D. Warner, editor. "Joel Chandler Harris," Volume XII, page 6961.

Orgain, Kate Alma. *Southern Authors in Poetry and Prose.* New York and Washington: Neale Publishing Co. 1908. 233 pages. "Joel Chandler Harris," pages 110-118.

Pickett, LaSalle Corbell ("Mrs. G. E. Pickett"). *Literary Hearthstones of Dixie.* Philadelphia and London: J. B. Lippincott Co. 1912. 304 pages. "Uncle Remus—Joel Chandler Harris," pages 151-172.

Reed, Wallace Putnam, editor. *History of Atlanta, Georgia.* Syracuse, N. Y.: D. Mason & Co. 1889. 491 pages. "Joel Chandler Harris," pages 413-419.

Rutherford, Mildred Lewis. *American Authors.* Atlanta, Ga.: Franklin Printing Co. 1894. 750 pages. "Joel Chandler Harris," pages 610-614.

Rutherford, Mildred Lewis. *The South in History and Literature.* Atlanta, Ga.: Franklin-Turner Co. 1907. 866 pages. "Joel Chandler Harris," pages 505-509.

Smith, Charles Alphonso. *Die Amerikanische Literatur.* Berlin: Weidmann. 1912.

Smith, Charles Alphonso. *Cambridge History of American Literature.* Published uniformly with the Cambridge English Literature Series. A chapter on Harris by C. Alphonso Smith.

South in the Building of the Nation, The. Richmond, Va.: Southern Historical Publication Society. 1913. "Joel Chandler Harris." See Index, Volume XIII., page 89.

Toulmin, Harry Aubrey. *Social Historians.* Boston: R. G. Badger.

1911. 176 pages. "Bibliography," pages 167-171. "Joel Chandler Harris," pages 133-164.

Trent, William Peterfield. *Southern Writers.* New York: Macmillan. 1905.

Watterson, Henry. *Oddities in Southern Life and Character.* Boston: Houghton. 1882.

Wootten, Katherine Hinton. *Bibliography of the Works of Joel Chandler Harris.* In Carnegie Library of Atlanta *Bulletin,* May-June, 1907.

Wright, Henrietta Christian. *Children's Stories in American Literature, 1660-1890.* New York: C. Scribner's Sons. 1895-96. Two volumes. "Joel Chandler Harris," Volume II., pages 153-162.

MAGAZINE ARTICLES ABOUT HARRIS

Adair, Forrest, "Joel Chandler Harris." *American Illustrated Methodist Magazine,* October, 1899; Volume XI., page 124.

Anonymous. "The Snap-bean Sage," *Saturday Review of Literature,* May, 1925, page 721.

Arms, Ethel. "Leaves from a Reporter's Notebook." Interview with Joel Chandler Harris. *National Magazine,* Boston, February, 1905; Volume XXI., pages 515-517.

"Author of 'Uncle Remus'." *American Review of Reviews,* August, 1908; Volume XXXVIII., pages 214-215.

Avary, Mrs. Myrta (Lockett). "The 'Wren's Nest' Preserved as a Memorial." *Book News Monthly,* May, 1913; Volume XXXI., pages 665-668.

Baker, Ray Standard. "Joel Chandler Harris." *Outlook,* November 5, 1904; Volume LXXVIII., pages 594-603.

Ball, Sumter Mays, "Joel Chandler Harris." *Book News Monthly,* January, 1909; Volume XXVII., pages 311-316.

Baskervill, William Malone. "Joel Chandler Harris." *Chautauquan,* October, 1896; Volume XXIV., pages 62-67.

"Brer Rabbit and Mr. Fox as Footlight Favorites in London." *Current Opinion,* July, 1914; Volume LVII., page 30.

Brown, Calvin S., Jr. Sketch. *Christian Advocate,* Nashville, Tenn., October 17, 1891.

Brown, W. N. "The Tar-Baby at Home," *Scientific Monthly,* 15 July-December, 1922. 228-234.

Christian Work, New York. Sketch. September 27, 1894.

Coleman, Charles W. "The Recent Movement in Southern Literature." *Harper's New Monthly Magazine*, May, 1887; Volume LXXIV., pages 844-848.

Crane, T. F. "Plantation Folklore." *Popular Science Monthly*, April, 1881; Volume XVIII., pages 824-833.

Ellis, Leonora B. "Harris and the Children." *Book News Monthly*, January, 1909; Volume XXVII., pages 321-323.

English, Thomas H. "In Memory of Uncle Remus." *Southern Literary Messenger*, 2 February, 1940; pages 77-83.

Espinosa, Aurelio. "Notes on the History of the Tar-Baby." *JAFL*, April-June, 1943; pages 129-209.

"First Stories of Uncle Remus." *Current Literature*, December, 1900; Volume XXIX., pages 708-709.

Garnsey, John Henderson. "Joel Chandler Harris: A Character Sketch." *Book Buyer*, March, 1896; New Series, Volume XIII., pages 65-68.

Gerber, A. "Uncle Remus Traced to the Old World." *Journal of American Folklore*, October-December, 1893; Volume VI., page 245.

Harman, Henry E. "Joel Chandler Harris." *Bookman*, 61 March, 1925. 433-436.

Harris, Joel Chandler. "An Accidental Author." Literary autobiography. *Lippincott's Monthly Magazine*, April, 1886; Volume XXXVII., pages 417-420.

Harris, Julia Collier. "Joel Chandler Harris: The Poetic Mind." *Emory University Quarterly*, March, 1947.

Harris, Julia Collier. "Uncle Remus at Home and Abroad." *Southern Literary Messenger*, February, 1940, pages 84-86.

Harris, Mrs. L. H. "The Passing of 'Uncle Remus'." *Independent*, July 23, 1908; Volume LXV., pages 190-192.

Hawthorne, H. "Teller of Folk and Fairy Tales." *St. Nicholas*, March, 1915; Volume XLII., pages 453-455.

Horton, Mrs. Thaddeus. "The Most Modest Author in America." *Ladies Home Journal*, May, 1907; Volume XXIV., page 17. Also in *The Atlanta Constitution*, May 5, 1907.

"How Joel Chandler Harris Came to Write the Uncle Remus Stories." *Current Literature*, August, 1908; Volume V., page 164.

Hubbell, J. B. "Letters of Uncle Remus." *Southwest Review*, xxiii, January, 1938. 216-223.

"Joel Chandler Harris." *Nation,* July 9, 1908; Volume LXXXVII., pages 30, 31.

Knight, Lucian Lamar. "Uncle Remus." (See "Men and Women of the Craft." *Bohemian Magazine,* Easter, 1901. Fort Worth, Texas)

Lee, J. W. "Joel Chandler Harris." *Century Magazine,* April, 1909; Volume LXXVII., pages 891-897.

"Letter to President Roosevelt and His Response." *Uncle Remus's the Home Magazine,* September, 1908; Volume XXIV., pages 5, 6.

McClurg, Alexander C. "Old Time Plantation Life: On the Plantation." *Review.* Dial (Chicago), June, 1892; Volume XIII., pages 46-49.

McQueen, A. "Teller of Tales." Poem. *Lippincott's Monthly Magazine,* October, 1911; Volume LXXXVIII., page 543.

Marquis, Don. "The Farmer of Snap Bean Farm." *Uncle Remus's the Home Magazine,* September, 1908; Volume XXIV, page 7.

Merriam, Mrs. M. F. "At Snap Bean Farm." *Southern Ruralist,* October 15, 1913; Volume XIX., page 22.

Parsons, Elsie Clews. "Joel Chandler Harris and Negro Folklore." *The Dial,* 66. May, 1919, 491-493.

Pickett, L. C. "Uncle Remus." *Lippincott's Monthly Magazine,* April, 1912. Volume LXXXIX., pages 572-578.

Reed, Wallace Putnam. "Joel Chandler Harris, Humorist and Novelist." *Literature,* October 27, 1888.

Rice, Grantland; Thomas E. Watson; Frank L. Stanton. Tributes to Joel Chandler Harris. *Uncle Remus's Home Magazine,* September, 1908; Volume XXIV., p. 8.

Stovall, Genie O. Sketch quoting Mr. Harris in regard to his early life. *Children's Visitor,* November 23, 1902.

Ticknor, Caroline. "Glimpses of the Author of 'Uncle Remus'." *Bookman,* August, 1908; Volume XXVII., pages 551-557.

Ticknor, Caroline. "The Man Harris: A Study in Personality." *Book News Monthly,* January, 1909. Volume XXVII., pages 317-320.

"Uncle Remus." Review of book. *Nation,* December 2, 1880; Volume XXXI., page 398.

"Uncle Remus." Review of book. *Public Opinion,* March 26, 1881; Volume XXXIX., page 391.

"Uncle Remus." Review of book. *Spectator,* April 2, 1881; Volume LIV., pages 445, 446.

"Uncle Remus." On the death of Mr. Harris. *Nation,* July 9, 1908; Volume LXXXVII., pages 26, 27.

"Uncle Remus." *Harper's Weekly,* July 11, 1908; Volume LII., page 29.

"Uncle Remus." *South Atlantic Quarterly,* October, 1908.

"Young Minstrels." *Collier's Weekly,* September 19, 1914; Volume LIV., page 10.

NEWSPAPER ARTICLES ABOUT HARRIS

The Atlanta Constitution. "The Constitutional Staff." "S. S.," in the the Philadelphia Evening *Telegram.* "Old Si" and "Uncle Remus" contrasted in personal appearance, etc. March 22, 1879.

The Atlanta Constitution. "Uncle Remus in Brief." April 20, 1879.

The Atlanta Constitution. Mrs. Thaddeus Horton. "The Most Modest Author in America." May 5, 1907.

The Atlanta Constiution. Fred Lewis. "Some Incidents and Characteristics of Uncle Remus." October 7, 1906, page 3.

The Atlanta Constitution. "Joel Chandler Harris Summoned by the Master of All Good Workmen." July 4, 1908; Volume XLI., pages 1, 6.

The Atlanta Constitution. "Letter to Miss Katharine Wootten," Carnegie Library, Atlanta, to thank her for the preparation of a bibliography of the works of Uncle Remus. Dated September 17, 1907. Signed Joel Chandler Harris. July 4, 1908; Volume XLI., page 6. Letter is in Carnegie Library of Atlanta *Bulletin,* May-June, 1907.

Atlanta *Georgian and News.* July 4, 1908. Sketch.

Boston *Globe.* November 3, 1907. James B. Morrow. "Mr. Harris Talks of His Life."

Boston *Post.* Correspondence from "Atlanta, Georgia, September 28, 1881." Walter H. Page.

Memphis *Commercial-Appeal.* Mrs. Robert L. Spain. "Uncle Remus and Snap Bean Farm." November 15, 1908.

New York *Times.* "New Edition of 'Uncle Remus'." October 16, 1895.

New York *World.* Description of home and family. December 4, 1892.

London *Times.* "Joel Chandler Harris." July 6, 1908, page 8.

BOOKS REFERRED TO IN THE NOTES

Anonymous. *75 Years of Freedom.* Washington, D. C., 1940.

Beckwith, Martha Warren. *Jamaican Folk-Lore.* New York, 1928.

Blair, Walter. *Native American Humor.* New York, 1937.
Botkin, B. A. *A Treasury of American Folklore.* New York, 1944.
Brawley, Benjamin G. *A Short History of the American Negro.* New York, 1927.
Brewer, J. Mason. *Humorous Folk Tales of the South Carolina Negro.* Orangeburg, S. C., 1945.
Brown, Sterling; Davis, Arthur; Lee, Ulysses. *The Negro Caravan.* New York, 1941.
Dubois, W. E. B. *The Gift of Black Folk.* New York, 1924.
Gaines, F. P. *The Southern Plantation.* New York, 1925.
Harris, Julia Collier. *The Life and Letters of Joel Chandler Harris.* Boston, 1918.
Harris, Julia Collier. *Joel Chandler Harris, Editor and Essayist.* Chapel Hill, N. C., 1931.
Hulme, F. E. *Proverb Lore.* London, 1902.
Hurston, Zora Neale. *Mules and Men.* Philadelphia, 1935.
Jackson, George Pullen. *White and Negro Spirituals.* New York, 1943.
Jekyll, Walter. *Jamaican Song and Story.* London, 1907.
Johnson, James Weldon. *The Book of American Negro Poetry.* New York, 1922.
Jones, Charles C. Jr. *Negro Myths of the Georgia Coast.* Boston, 1888.
Krappe, Alexander. *The Science of Folklore.* London, 1930.
Lanier, Sidney. *The Science of English Verse.* New York, 1880.
Locke, Alain. *The New Negro.* New York. 1925.
Lomax, John A. and Lomax, Alan. *American Ballads and Folk Songs.* New York, 1934.
Macon, John Alfred. *Uncle Gabe Tucker, or Reflection, Song, and Sentiment in the Quarters.* Philadelphia, 1883.
Nelson, John Herbert. *The Negro Character in American Literature.* Lawrence, Kansas, 1926.
Odum, H. W. and Johnson, G. B. *The Negro and His Songs.* Chapel Hill, N. C., 1926.
Pattee, Fred Lewis. *American Literature Since 1870.* New York, 1915.
Puckett, Newbell Niles. *Folk Beliefs of the Southern Negro.* Chapel Hill, N. C., 1926.
Scarborough, Dorothy. *On the Trail of Negro Folk Songs.* Cambridge, Mass., 1925.
Talley, Thomas W. *Negro Folk Rhymes.* New York, 1922.
Thompson, Harold W. *Body, Boots, and Britches.* Philadelphia, 1940.

Thompson, Stith. *Motif—Index of Folk-Literature.* Bloomington, Indiana, 1932.

Thompson, Stith. *Tales of North American Indians,* Cambridge, Mass., 1929.

Taylor, Archer. *The Proverb.* Cambridge, Mass., 1931.

White, Newman I. *American Negro Folk Songs.* Cambridge, Mass., 1928.

Wiggins, R. L. *The Life of Joel Chandler Harris.* Nashville, Tennessee, 1918.

Williams, John G. *De Ole Plantation.* Charleston, S. C., 1895.

Work, J. W. *Folk Songs of the American Negro.* Nashville, Tenn., 1915.

NOTES

CHAPTER I

1. Joel Chandler Harris, *Uncle Remus, His Songs and His Sayings,* 1895 edition (New York, 1880), pp. iii, iv.

2. Julia Collier Harris, *The Life and Letters of Joel Chandler Harris* (Boston and New York, 1918) and *Joel Chandler Harris, Editor and Essayist* (Chapel Hill, 1931.

3. Lucien Harris and Mr. and Mrs. Julian Harris have supplied the following biographical facts. See "Significant Dates in the Life of Joel Chandler Harris," *The Southern Literary Messenger,* (February, 1940), 76. December 9, 1848, born in Eatonton, Georgia, 1861: began apprenticeship to printer on only newspaper ever published on a plantation, the *Countryman,* Joseph Addison Turner of 'Turnwold', owner. His first writings published in it anonymously. 1864-65: printer on Macon *Telegraph.* 1866-67: private secretary to editor of the *Crescent Monthly* of New Orleans that published his verse. 1867: on Monroe *Advertiser* (Ga.). 1870: associate editor Savannah *Morning News.* April 21, 1873: married Esther La Rose. They had nine children. 1875: Lucien Harris born (Living in Atlanta). 1876: became an editorial paragrapher and telegraph editor on the *Atlanta Constitution* and created "Uncle Remus." Remained on the editorial staff of this newspaper for twenty-five years. 1880: *Uncle Remus: His Songs and His Sayings.* 1907: *Uncle Remus's Magazine* issued with his son, Julian (later consolidated with the *Home Magazine*). July 3, 1908: Joel Chandler Harris died in "The Wren's Nest," his home in Atlanta, Ga. July 5, 1908: buried in Westview Cemetery, Atlanta, Ga.

4. *Life and Letters,* p. 23.

5. *The Atlanta Constitution,* May 18, 1877.

6. Joel Chandler Harris, *On The Plantation* (New York, 1892), pp. 27-31.

7. *Ibid.,* p. 33.

8. *Ibid.,* p. 156.

9. Joel Chandler Harris, "An Accidental Author," *Lippincott's Magazine,* XXXVII (April, 1886), pp. 418-419.

10. Jay B. Hubbell, "Letters of Uncle Remus," *Southwest Review,* XXIII (January, 1938). p. 220.

11. Harris, "An Accidental Author," p. 419.

12. *Life and Letters,* pp. 36, 37.

13. *Editor and Essayist,* p. 96n.

14. *The Atlanta Constitution,* November 30, 1879.

15. *On the Plantation,* p. 22.

16. Joel Chandler Harris, "Introduction," to *Poems by Irwin Russell* (New York, 1888), pp. X-XI.

17. "An Accidental Author," p. 419.

18. See Appendix for the complete article.

19. Joel Chandler Harris in *The Atlanta Constitution,* December 9, 1877.

20. *Life and Letters,* p. 97.

21. *Ibid.*

22. *Ibid.*
23. *Ibid*, p. 98.
24. *Ibid.*
25. *Editor and Essayist*, p. 113.
26. *Life and Letters*, p. 144.
27. *Ibid.* p. 143.

CHAPTER II

1. Fred Lewis Pattee, *American Literature Since 1870* (New York, 1915), p. 306.
2. *Life and Letters*, p. 162.
3. *Ibid.*, p. 153.
4. *Ibid.*, p. 161.
5. *Ibid.*, p. 154.
6. *Ibid.*, pp. 155-158.
7. *Songs and Sayings*, p. 25.
8. *Life and Letters*, p. 149.
9. *Ibid.*, p. 150.
10. *Ibid.*, p. 334.
11. *Songs and Sayings*, pp. vii-ix.
12. Professor of Geology at Cornell University.
13. *Songs and Sayings*, p. xi.
14. *Life and Letters*, p. 192.
15. *Ibid.*, 192-193.
16. Mr. Jones' book was *Negro Myths of the Georgia Coast*, published in 1888.
17. *Life and Letters*, p. 195.
18. W. H. I. Bleek, *Reynard, the Fox, in South Africa; or Hottentot Fables and Tales.*
19. Joel Chandler Harris, *Nights with Uncle Remus* (Boston, 1883), p. XXXV.
20. Caroline Tichnor, "Glimpses of the Author of Uncle Remus," *Bookman*, XXVII (August, 1908), p. 554.
21. *Songs and Sayings*, p. 10.
22. *Nights with Uncle Remus*, p. xiv.
23. *Ibid*, p. xv.
24. Joel Chandler Harris, *Uncle Remus and His Friends* (Boston, 1892), p. iv.
25. Youngster referred to was Julian La Rose Harris.
26. *Uncle Remus and His Friends*, p. vi.
27. *Ibid.*, p. vii.
28. *Life and Letters*, pp. 299-300.
29. Hubbell, "Letters of Uncle Remus," pp. 216-223.
30. *Life and Letters*, p. 455.
31. *Uncle Remus and His Friends*, pp. 10-11.
32. *Life and Letters*, pp. 393-395.
33. *Ibid.*, pp. 384-386.
34. *Ibid.*, p. 197.
35. *Songs and Sayings*, p. 119.
36. *Life and Letters*, p. 168.
37 *Ibid.*, pp. 169-170.

CHAPTER III

1. *Songs and Sayings*, p. vii.
2. *Life and Letters*, p. 570.
3. *Ibid.*
4. *Ibid.*
5. *Songs and Sayings*, p. xvii.
6. *Ibid.*, p. 3-4.
7. *Nights with Uncle Remus*, pp. 382, 134.
8. Julia Collier Harris remarks that Mr. J. T. Manry who worked with Mr. Harris on the *Monroe Advertiser* at Forsyth, Georgia, was of the opinion that the name Uncle Remus was a souvenir of Forsyth days. "The 'town gardener' . . . was called Uncle Remus and Mr. Manry recalls that the . . . name appealed to father's imagination at that time." See *Life and Letters*, p. 146.
9. Pattee, *American Literature Since 1870*, p. 305.
10. *Nights with Uncle Remus*, p. 400.
11. Joel Chandler Harris, *Daddy Jake the Runaway, and Short Stories told After Dark* (New York, 1889), pp. 152-153.
12. Hubbell, "Letters of Uncle Remus" p. 222.
13. Earlier specimens of the type are found in *Anti-Fanaticism* (1855), *Home and the World* (1857), and *Maum Guinea's Children* (1861). See John Herbert Nelson, *The Negro Character in American Literature*, p. 110.
14. Joel Chandler Harris, *Uncle Remus Returns* (Boston, 1918), p. 79.
15. *Uncle Remus and His Friends*, p. 91.
16. *Daddy Jake the Runaway*, pp. 171-172.
17. *Ibid.*, p. 173.
18. *Nights with Uncle Remus*, p. 17.
19. *Uncle Remus and His Friends*, p. 101.
20. *Uncle Remus Returns*, p. 134.
21. *Ibid.*, p. 80.
22. *Nights with Uncle Remus*, pp. 132-133.
23. *Ibid.*, p. 147.
24. *Songs and Sayings*, p. v.
25. *Uncle Remus and His Friends*, p. x.
26. *Ibid.*, p. vii.
27. Joel Chandler Harris, *Told by Uncle Remus: New Stories of the Old Plantation* (New York, 1905), p. 4.
28. *Life and Letters*, p. 488.
30. *Ibid.*, p. 498n.
31. Thomas H. English, ed., "Seven Tales of Uncle Remus" (Emory University, 1948), p. 5.
32. *Ibid.*, p. 5.

CHAPTER IV

1. Adolf Gerber, "Uncle Remus Traced to the Old World," *JAFL* (January-March, 1893), p. 249.
2. Walter Jekyll, *Jamaican Song and Story* (London, 1907), pp. ix-xxxviii.

CHAPTER V

1. *Uncle Remus and His Friends*, p. 135.

2. For table giving name of animal cheated and name of story in which fraud occurs, see Appendix.

3. *Life and Letters*, p. 333.

CHAPTER VI

1. Stith Thompson, *Tales of North American Indians* (Cambridge, Massachussets, 1929), p. xvii.

2. Of this story Harris says: "This story is popular on the coast and among the rice-plantation and since the publication of some of the animal-myths in the newspapers, I have received a version of it from a planter in southwest Georgia; but it seems to me to be an intruder among the genuine myth-stories of the negroes. It is a trifle too elaborate. Nevertheless, it is told upon the plantations with great gusto, and there are several versions in circulation." Joel Chandler Harris, *S. and S.*, footnote, p. 156.

CHAPTER VII

1. *Nights with Uncle Remus*, p. 158.

2. A different version of "Taily-po" is found in B. A. Botkin, *Treasury of American Folklore* (New York, 1944), p. 679.

3. Zora Neale Hurston gives a version of this story in *Mules and Men.* In her story, the devil says, "Here, take dis hot coal and g'wan off and start you a hell uh yo' own."

A similar story is "Jacky-My-Lantern", a Maryland version appears in B. A. Botkin, *A Treasury of American Folklore*, p. 725.

4. *Uncle Remus Returns*, p. 50.

CHAPTER VIII

1. Archer Taylor, *The Proverb* (Cambridge, Massachussets, 1931), p. 3.

2. J. Mason Brewer, *Humorous Folk Lore Tales of the South Carolina Negro* (Orangeburg, South Carolina, 1945), p. 45.

3. Joseph Alfred Macon, *Uncle Gabe Tucker* or *Reflection, Song and Sentiment in the Quarters* (Philadelphia, 1883).

4. Martha Warren Beckwith has assembled 972 in her *Jamaican Folk-Lore* (New York, 1928), and Frank Candall has a collection of 1383 in *Jamaica Negro Proverbs and Sayings* (Kingston, 1910).

5. Harold W. Thompson, *Body, Boots and Britches* (Philadelphia, 1940), p. 482.

6. *Ibid.*, p. 493.

7. *Ibid.*, p. 501.

8. *Ibid.*, p. 482. See proberb: "It's just as 'tis, and tain't no 'tis-er."

9. *Songs and Sayings*, p. 149-152.

CHAPTER IX

1. *Life and Letters*, p. 215.

2. *Ibid.*

3. *Songs and Sayings*, pp. vii-viii.

4. *Ibid.*, p. xvi.

5. *Nights with Uncle Remus,* p. xxxii.

6. John G. Williams, *De Ole Plantation* (Charleston, 1895), p. xi.

7. *Ibid.,* p. xiii.

8. See C. Alphonso Smith in *The Cambridge History of American Literature,* II (New York, 1918), pp. 358-359.

9. *Nights with Uncle Remus,* pp. xxxii-xxxiv.

10. *Uncle Remus and His Friends,* pp. viii, ix.

11. *Cambridge History of American Literature,* II, p. 358.

12. *Life and Letters,* pp. 403-404.

13. *Ibid.,* p. 164.

14. Julia Collier Harris, "Uncle Remus at Home and Abroad," in *Southern Literary Messenger,* Volume II (February, 1940), p. 85.

15. Mrs. Thaddeus Horton, "The Most Modest Author in America," *Ladies Home Journal,* Vol. XXIV (May, 1907), p. 17.

16. See *Life and Letters,* pp. 164-165.

CHAPTER X

1. *Songs and Sayings,* pp. xv-xvi.

2. Joel Chandler Harris, *Tar-Baby and Other Rhymes of Uncle Remus* (New York, 1904). See Author's note.

3. Alain Locke, in "*75 Years of Freedom, Commemoration of the 75th Anniversary of the Proclamation of the 13th Amendment to the Constitution of the United States,*" (Washington, 1940), p. 10.

4. *Songs and Sayings,* p. 193.

5. John A. and Alan Lomax, *American Ballads and Folk Songs* (New York, 1934), p. 20.

6. J. Mason Brewer has a story in "Juneteenth" which gives a similar idea.

7. Alain Locke, in "*75 Years of Freedom,*" p. 12, wrote: "The frequency of the reference to Jordan has always interested me greatly. While I know the importance of that in the Christian tradition and the way it would naturally fasten itself on the mind of slave groups, especially those that were used to the ritual of baptism, I personally think that there is back of this some of that primitive carry-over water symbolism of the West African religions."

8. *Uncle Remus and His Friends,* p. 211.

9. *Ibid.,* p. 201.

10. "In a letter to the poet, Paul Hamilton Hayne (year not given), in reference to a selection from the 'Ballads' for an anthology, father said: 'I would suggest "The Plough-Hands' Song" as perhaps the most characteristic!" Julia Collier Harris *Life and Letters,* p. 185.

11. *Uncle Remus and His Friends,* p. 193.

12. Sterling Brown, Arthur Davis, Ulysses Lee, *The Negro Caravan* (New York, 1941), p. 422.

13. *Uncle Remus and His Friends,* p. 203.

14. *On the Plantation,* pp. 19, 80.

15. Julia Collier Harris wrote: "Of the ballads written during 1882-83, and collected in the *Uncle Remus* volume of 1892, father's favorite was the one called

'O, Gimme de Gal' . . . the song's realism is the very quality that makes it a cotton-field classic." *Life and Letters,* p. 185n.

16. Thomas W. Talley, *Negro Folk Rhymes* (New York, 1922), p. 313.

17. See Dorothy Scarborough, *On the Trail of Negro Folk Songs* (Cambridge, 1925), pp. 145-147.

18. *Uncle Remus and His Friends,* p. 197.

19. Scarborough, *Op. Cit.,* p. 23.

20. Talley, *Op. Cit.,* p. 25.

21. *Ibid.,* p. 236.

22. *Ibid.,* pp. 312-313.

23. *Songs and Sayings,* p. 195.

24. Scarborough, p. 165.

25. Talley, p. 122.

26. Brown, Davis, and Lee, *The Negro Caravan,* p. 422.

27. Scarborough, p. 165.

28. Talley, p. 5.

29. Alfred J. Swan, "Eight Negro Songs from Bedford County, Virginia." (Collected by Francis Abbott).

30. Talley, p. 242.

31. *Ibid.,* p. 265.

32. *Nights with Uncle Remus,* pp. 72-73.